Great Escapes

The Spring Breaker's Guide to Beaches and Beyond

by

Ann Schimke

First Edition

Cover Design by Bremmer & Goris
Typesetting by Edington-Rand
Illustrations by Paul A. Michalak

Care and diligence have been taken in organizing and presenting the information contained in *Great Escapes*, however, Octameron does not guarantee its accuracy.

Address editorial correspondence to:
Octameron Associates, Inc.
P.O. Box 2748
Alexandria, VA 22301
703/836-5480
www.octameron.com

Address bookstore inquiries regarding purchases and returns to:
Dearborn Trade
155 North Wacker Drive
Chicago, IL 60606
Outside Illinois, 800/245-BOOK
In Illinois, 312/836-4400 x270

ISBN 1-057509-031-1

PRINTED IN THE UNITED STATES OF AMERICA

Table of Contents

Part II   Slopeside Breaks

Part III Trail Breaks

Part IV Spring Break Alternatives

6 Contents

'Twas the Night Before Spring Break

It's midnight. The library is packed with frantic midterm crammers. You are one of them, dressed to the nines in crumpled sweats, surrounded by text books, lecture notes and empty Coke cans. Your last midterm is tomorrow morning, will you make it? You start to feel delirious. Your notes begin to blur, the walls of your carrel begin closing in, you look around at your fellow students and see only pod people. Things aren't going so well.

Before you go catatonic, take a deep breath. Remember, spring break is only a day away. Quick! Rehash your plans! It's the only thing that will get you through. So, you're going to bolt back to the dorm after the test, grab your bag, meet up with the gang and bust this town, right?

What? No spring break plans? What were you doing in December and January when you should have been plotting your spring escape? Surely not studying. Alas, it's never too early to start planning next year's trip. Below are a few suggestions to get you in the spring break state of mind.

Go South, Young Man (and Woman!)

Are you aching to leave those dirty snow banks and salt-stained shoes behind? Well, fuel up and head south! Numerous warm 'n sunny destinations await. In addition to Florida's celebrated break cities, the state-side crew can count on various locales in Texas and Arizona for a properly raucous spring break. If you're willing to venture outside the U.S. (and spend a few extra dollars), you'll find plenty of sun-dappled beaches in Mexico and the Caribbean on which to sprawl. So strip down to your skivvies and get ready to frolic with the masses. (Don't go questing after solitude and serenity at a major break location, you won't find it!) By day, you'll become a stitch in the crazy quilt of colorful beach towels, florescent bikinis and trunks, and glinting beer cans. You'll laze on the sand, dip in the ocean, maybe even try your hand at wind surfing or jet skiing. By night, you'll dance yourself silly in a crush of happy-go-lucky breakers.

Snow Goose Getaways

So you want to feel crisp, cold mountain air on your face and the adrenaline in your veins this spring break? Forget the sun roof, you better break out the roof rack, and your skies or snowboard too. This is no time for a rushed half-day ski trip sandwiched between three hour driving stints. You've earned a full-fledged ski vacation. Since much of the country is still under snow in March, you shouldn't have any trouble finding an inviting lodge or resort where you can schuss and ride to your heart's content. At night, you'll soak your aches away in the hot tub, or at least a hot shower, then you and your fellow ski bunnies can hit the bars, clubs and coffeehouses that grace any respectable ski-town. Rest assured budget-conscious students, many resorts have spring break specials on lift tickets and rentals or, at least, student discounts. Pack yourself and your ten best friends into a bungalow, and lodging won't wipe you out either.

Trail Blazing Breaks

So, you'd give anything to get outside and stay there this spring break? It sounds like you've been cooped up in that closet they call a dorm room a little too long. Here's betting that you yearn for the smell of smoke in your flannel, the taste of strong coffee brewed over a camp stove and the sight of a star-spattered night sky. Well, deprive yourself no longer! Chuck those sleeping bags and backpacks in the trunk, buy some trail mix and some ramen and head for the wild blue yonder. There are hundreds of state and national parks to visit, dozens of which lie in the country's warmer southern climes. You'll climb mountains, forge rivers and cross deserts. Boring, processed food will never have tasted so good, and sleep will never have seemed so refreshing. Sure, you'll get a little grungy, but if there's no dirt, you won't be roughing it.

Escaping the Ivory Tower

Despite the stress of imminent term papers and exams, let's face it, college life engenders a certain amount of idyll and ease. You can't get fired, and hey, it's not like world peace is hanging in the balance over your sociology grade. And if you think it is, it's time to hop the ivy walls and get involved; get your hands dirty helping real people with real world problems. That's what Alternative Spring Break is all about. Hundreds of schools offer these week-long service trips, during which students do everything from building houses for low-income families to planting trees in deforested areas. As an alternative breaker, you'll get up early and work hard all day. Often times you'll sleep in YMCA dorms or church halls. Still many students say no other spring break experience brings such great rewards. Besides making a difference in other peoples' lives, you'll bond with your cronies, learn new skills, and shatter stereotypes you didn't even know you had.

Calling All Road Warriors

Feeling a little peripatetic? Like you'd rather not spend your precious spring break rooted in one place. Sounds like you, in high college tradition, are hankering for a road trip. It's a good thing the country's big and gas is cheap. Dig out that dog-eared travel atlas, grab a couple friends and hit the nearest highway on-ramp. The beauty of road tripping is that you can cover as much or little distance as you like. This means you can have your New Orleans jambalaya and your friends can have their Graceland kitsch too. All you need is a reliable vehicle and a love of the road. Remember, if you don't indulge your whimsy now, pretty soon you'll find yourself stuck in a job with hardly enough vacation time to go home for the holidays, let alone travel cross-country.

Lots O' Other Stuff

So, you haven't hit on a spring break idea yet? Well, before you resign yourself to a week of Doom-playing and Seinfeld-watching, check out these off-the-beaten-track options: If college sports haven't drained all the rah-rah out of you, how about cheering for your favorite baseball team during spring training in Florida or Arizona? Are you looking for serenity and a little time to reflect? How about a meditation retreat in the Ozark Mountains? Craving some hip musical fare? Try an alternative tune-fest in Austin or Toronto? Studying abroad for a semester? Hit the rails and see the world. Whatever you do this spring break, give yourself a week to remember.

Found a Hole?

So you went to a super cool spring break spot and found no mention of it in this book? Don't leave us hanging! Let us know where you went and what you did. We want *Great Escapes* to be the definitive guide to spring break, and we won't be happy until it is. Also, if you have a brief (150-250 words) spring break story to tell, we'd like to hear it. We've included several "student anecdotes" in this edition and will be seeking new ones for our 2nd edition, to be published in September 1998.

Please forward any comments or contributions to:

Octameron Associates
Great Escapes
P.O. Box 2748
Alexandria, VA 22301

Part One **Beach Breaks**

A Blast From the Past

If you're not going home this spring break, chances are, you're going to the beach; you and several hundred thousand of your peers. You'll hit Panama City, Daytona Beach, Fort Lauderdale, Key West, South Padre Island and Lake Havasu. You'll tan, you'll drink, you'll dance and you'll scope. You might take a bungee plunge or ride the waves on a jet ski. You might just laze on the sand and play volleyball all week. Whatever your preference, you'll find out everything you need to know in the next 5 chapters.

How It All Started

Even early in the century, college students went south for spring break. Of course, trips to the beaches and mineral springs were reserved for affluent students, and by nature of the college population, mostly men. Over the years, however, spring break grew into a more equitable and rambunctious institution. As more colleges went co-ed, female students joined the mix, and as a result, spring break became a more scintillating, and thus more popular affair.

What really launched spring break though, was Hollywood, with the 1960 film *Where the Boys Are*. Young audiences were quickly enchanted by suave George Hamilton and pert Connie Francis, and spring break soon became a fixture in the popular imagination. The hitch-hiker's sign in one early scene said it all: "Ft. Lauderdale or I'll kill myself." The sentiment struck a chord with northern college students and many couldn't wait to flit down to Florida and fall in love, or at least drink and be merry.

Spring Break Stories: Fort Lauderdale, 1967

At the end of Winter Term, in early April, 1967, six of us piled into Gary Somebody-From-Detroit's little Plymouth and made our way to Fort Lauderdale. We had no where to stay, so we crashed on the beaches in front of different hotels each night. We showered at the outdoor public showers housed in the lifeguard office at the corner of Route A1A and Las Olas Boulevard, the very heart of the action in Fort Lauderdale.

In just a few days, the population of that little area went up somewhere between ten and thirty thousand. I'd have to see an old newspaper to know for sure, but it was unbelievable.

The Miami Herald set up its cameras on top of the public shower building, to record for posterity the tens of thousands of college kids going berserk on the beach...solid bodies from the street to the water, as far as you could see either way. We were on our blankets right there in the middle of it all, with me playing guitar and all of us singing the songs that had so effectively chased girls away since we were thrown into Snyder Hall dormitory at Michigan State in the fall of 1966.

Of course, these flaming college guys see cameras, so they start trying to climb the palm trees near the shower building. The guys are all drunk, and they're grabbing the palm trees in a bear hug and trying to shinny up the trees, scraping the crap out of their chests and legs on the sharp, coarse bark. And, even worse, when they got tired and gave up, they'd loosen their grip a little and *sslliide* all the way down, ripping themselves to shreds.

So my good buddy, Chris Hoffman, a delightful, handsome rich kid from Birmingham, and Carl Dincesen, the 16-year old drummer from my high school band, start egging me on. "Come on Martling, you're a monkey, you could get up that tree." Of course I could. I was still in shape from high school gymnastics, and I was bombed ...the perfect combination. I proceeded to bend over and grunt my way through the crowd like an ape.

When I got to the tree, I reach around it, enough to hold on, but at arms length, and jumped onto the tree with a bare foot parallel to the ground on each side. In a squat, I zipped up the tree like my family forgot to evolve. When I reached the top, I held on tight and swung my legs out in celebration. The photographer got his shot, and it ran the next day on the front page with the story about the "College Invasion."

We never saw the picture until somebody sent one to us, long after we got back to school. And man, do I love it!"

Jackie "The Jokeman" Martling
Michigan State University '71
East Lansing, Michigan

Today, Jackie makes his living as a comedian and maintains the JokeLand web page at http://www.jokeland.com.

In the seventies, spring break continued to rage along on its deeply cut course, sticking with such stand-bys as Lauderdale and Daytona. Beer was king and most students, in their own "Staying Alive," Brady-haired way, wanted nothing more than a clean-cut good time.

You Gotta Fight For Your Right to Party

Although there wasn't much holding spring breakers back by the time the eighties rolled around, the classic Beastie Boys anthem sounded good anyway. Things got rowdy and "Me" decade breakers became notorious for picking fights with toilets, televisions and other troublesome hotel appliances.

The MTV Influence

The all-music network made its debut in 1981, but didn't get around to throwing its first spring break pool party until 1986. Right from the start, MTV (http://www.mtv.com/) and spring break were a match made in heaven. After all, who would more willingly embrace MTV than a bunch of junior hedonists hungry for easy-to-process entertainment? And who better to entertain such a crowd than the people who invented the bite-sized broadcast and made slackerdom cool.

Daytona Beach was MTV's first and longest spring break sweet heart, hosting the network every year between 1986 and 1993. The event was a mixed blessing for Daytona. On one hand, students came in droves, filling the coffers of local hotel owners and merchants. On the other hand, these visitors came hell-bent on a real MTV-style party. They wanted the whole nine-course shebang and they got it. There were big-name bands, popular veejays and flavor-of-the-month celebrities. Unfortunately, the rush that went along with all the merry-making reduced some breakers to rogues. They trashed hotel rooms, flouted social standards and generally caused a ruckus.

By 1993, the relationship had soured. Daytona blamed MTV for the trashy course that spring break had taken. MTV simply went looking for another patron. In 1994, MTV took the show to San Diego. In 1995, it chose Lake Havasu, Arizona. In 1996, the nomadic wandering ceased and MTV settled in Panama City, Florida. There it's stayed for the last two years, and as the town doesn't seem to mind the March mayhem, the network may stay for a couple more. (MTV officially announces its spring break site each December.)

Be a Star

Forget "I want my MTV." Today's breakers don't just want it, they want to be on it. And it's actually not that hard. MTV broadcasts many of it regular shows on location at Spring Break and regularly snaps up students to people the sets. The dating show, Singled Out, is a particular favorite among breakers, who can win a place as a contestant, card-holder or cheerleader. Best of all, Singled Out is shot in several "satellite" spring break cities as well as in MTV's Spring Break headquarter city. The Grind, MTV's update of American Band Stand, is another "interactive" show popular with students. Breakers can audition to dance on the show at whatever club is hosting MTV for spring break. Those who make the cut will have the pleasure of shaking their booties to the beat of bands like the Spice Girls.

MTV also showcases Love Line, Fame or Shame, MTV Jams and MTV Undercover during spring break. The last is a spring break version of "The Real World." MTV camera crews follow three college women and three college men through their spring break revelry and then broadcast it to voyeurs, umm viewers, across the nation.

The Diversification Decade

Spring break has slowly calmed down during the nineties. Yes, there is still lots of drunken cavorting, but it appears that the riotous mood of the 1980s has passed. Today, few hotel televisions live in fear of drowning in the pool and only the rare chair worries it will meet its maker on the parking lot pavement. (This is not to say, that most hotels won't still ask you for a $100 to $300 damage deposit, in cash. As the saying goes, once bitten, twice shy.)

Trotting to the Tropics

One reason spring break has mellowed is that students have begun spreading themselves out a little more. The lure of exotica has done its part to draw students away from the traditional

Florida and Texas destinations. Who can blame them for thinking Daytona Beach a tad provincial next to unknown tropical isles like Jamaica or the Bahamas? What's more, travel agencies have made it easy to go this route, with international travel packages costing little more than high-end domestic trips. Cancún in Mexico, Nassau in the Bahamas, and Montego Bay and Negril in Jamaica have proven to be the most popular international destinations and are the ones most often featured by tour operators.

The Growth of Alternatives

Planet beach has also lost a few spring breakers to the ski slopes, the backcountry and the community service sites of the Alternative Spring Break movement. Sure, there is still a critical mass on the beach, but diversification is the trend. Ski resorts got a boost with the influx of intense young snowboarders. National parks began hosting more breakers as extreme sports like mountain biking and rock climbing caught on. Alternative Spring Break was no doubt the dark horse of the bunch, coming up from nothing in the late eighties. Today, it is a small, but formidable 15,000 student affair, powered by the ideals of volunteerism and social justice.

General Spring Break Web Resources

Sun Shine Magazine
http://interoz.com/springbreak/
This spring break e-zine is a good place to read up on domestic and international beach destinations, including such off-the-beaten-path places as the Red Sea in Egypt. The site also includes a listing of spring break dates for hundreds of colleges.

SpringBreak.com
http://www.springbreak.com
When the construction dust settles, this site will feature a directory of spring break destinations and a list of spring break tour operators. Currently, it contains a "ride board" and a spring break store.

R&J's Spring Break Resource Page
http://ccwf.cc.utexas.edu/~guard/springbreak.htm
Created by two University of Texas students, this site contains
links to several popular beach destinations, information on hang-
over cures and tattoo removal and, of course, the proverbial
spring break photo essay.

Getting There

TWO

Your Car

*T*he *Junkmobile That Couldn't.* It's a familiar story. One minute you're cruising along in a heady state of road euphoria, the next you're standing at the side of the road waiting for a tow truck. While there's not much you can do about driving a clunker (you're a student after all), you can at least make sure the tow-truck's cheap.

Join the American Automobile Association (AAA). They'll bail you out if you break down, lock your keys in the car, get a flat tire or run out of gas. They'll also give you maps, travel guides and routing information. A one-year membership runs between $30 and $45. Call AAA at 1-800-962-4222.

Rental Cars

Many rental car agencies don't rent to people under 25. Those that do often tack on an extra $10 to $30 a day. It's these extra charges that make renting a car prohibitively expensive for students, as the base fee is usually quite reasonable. If you must rent a car, you'll probably find the best deals at small, regional rental agencies where the under-25 fees tend to be low. (Don't even bother calling Hertz or Avis.)

Maps

There are three ways to get maps for your spring break travels:

1. Buy them.
2. Get them free from AAA.
3. Download them off the web (for free). MapQuest (http://www.mapquest.com/) is the most comprehensive and user-friendly map site around. There, you can locate printable street maps, look up driving distances and get detailed directions to just about any destination in the U.S.

Student Advantage Card

Whether you're renting a car, buying a train or bus ticket, or booking a flight, you'll pay less with this card. Student Advantage Cards cost about $20 and are issued for each academic year starting in September. On Amtrak, you'll get a 15% discount, on Greyhound you'll get a 20% discount, at Dollar Rent-A-Car you'll get some part of the under-25 fee waived and at Delta Airlines you'll get a 10% discount. At most other airlines you will be eligible for a $10 to $20 discount. To order a Student Advantage Card call 1-800-96-AMTRAK.

By Commercial Bus

When it comes to bus travel, there are two certainties. The first is that the trip will take about twice as long as it would by car. The second is that you'll end up next to the coughing grandma, the drunk vagabond, the quarreling kids or the crying baby. (For a less cynical perspective on bus travel read Jack Kerouac's *On The Road*.) That said, buses are cheap and they go almost everywhere. Thus, for car-less spring breakers, they are often the most viable mode of transportation.

Greyhound Bus Lines stops in all the major spring break beach destinations in the U.S., including Panama City, Daytona Beach, Fort Lauderdale, Key West, South Padre Island and Lake Havasu. For ticket information call Greyhound at 1-800-231-2222 or check its web site at http://www.greyhound.com/.

By Train

Compared to bus travel, train travel is a breeze. It's more comfortable, speedier and best of all, usually involves a cafe car. But it's not what it used to be. Hard hit by funding cuts in recent years, Amtrak, the only government-subsidized passenger railway, has been forced to scrap dozens of routes and raise its fares. The only major spring break beach city it actually services is Fort Lauderdale. It comes within 25 miles of both Daytona Beach and Lake Havasu City, and within 60 and 125 miles of Panama City and South Padre Island respectively.

AAA members receive a 10% discount on most Amtrak fares. This discount cannot be used with the Student Advantage Card discount. For ticket information call Amtrak at 1-800-USA-RAIL or check its web site at http://www.amtrak.com/.

By Plane

Naturally, air travel reigns supreme in the quick-and-easy department. Still, it's expensive. Nevertheless, even paupers can fly once in awhile. The trick is to shop around (try small or regional carriers) and buy early (three to four months in advance.) If you still can't find an affordable ticket, try a consolidator company, or bucket shop as they're also known. These outfits buy large blocks of tickets wholesale and resell them for between 10% and 40% less than the regular fare. The catch is this: meandering routes, long layovers and bad seating assignments. Also, bucket shop tickets are not refundable. For a listing of bucket shops, scan the travel section of your Sunday paper.

Through a Tour Operator

Tour operators specialize in setting up trips, especially for groups. Their services range from booking hotel rooms to arranging every last detail of your trip from airport transfers to meals. Many students, especially those who go to international destinations, take their spring break trips through tour companies. The fact is, it's a whole lot easier this way, and it's not that expensive.

All-Inclusive Trips

A true all-inclusive trip, like its name indicates, includes everything. This means airfare, hotels, transfers to and from the airport, all meals and all drinks. Some packages include water sports and activities too. Generally, all-inclusives apply only to international destinations, though this is not to say that they are available for every international destination. Naturally, all-inclusive packages are more expensive, running about $250 to $300 more than packages that include just airfare and hotel. Still, you may find the convenience is well worth the expense. Most importantly, you won't run out of money, or if you do, you'll be assured of three squares and unlimited drink for the duration of your trip.

Since all-inclusive trips are typically offered by large, fancy hotels, room rates run high with these packages. In countries like

Mexico, where food can be extremely cheap, it may actually be less expensive to stay at a small, moderately priced hotel and dine out independently. For those who want something between all-inclusives and nothing at all, partial meal plans may be the answer. Many tour operators offer these plans, whereby students eat a certain number of meals, usually 7, at any of several designated restaurants outside of their hotels.

How to Earn a Free Trip

If you're motivated and responsible, but not so much so that you'd eschew a fun-fest in Florida, this could be the gig for you. Tour operators are always looking for "campus representatives" or "marketing interns" who can spare five or ten hours a week to put up posters, hand out fliers, place ads in the newspaper and otherwise promote that company's spring break program. Every time a student mails in one of the fliers you've posted or passed out, you'll get a commission. (Each flier contains your customer rep code.) After earning a certain number of commissions, usually 15 or 20, you'll receive a free trip. It's not an all-or-nothing proposition however. If, for example, you earn only half the commissions needed for a free trip, you'll pay only about half the trip price. If, on the other hand, you earn more commissions than you need, you can redeem the extras for cash.

Often, you don't even have to become a campus rep in order to earn a free trip. You can earn the required commissions simply by getting your fraternity, sorority, ultimate frisbee team or study group to sign up for a trip under your name. This means you'll be in charge of collecting the necessary documents and payment from your compadres, and hammering out the trip details with the tour operator.

Sniffing Out a Scam

Illegitimate or deceptive tour operators are the stuff of spring break nightmares: You get to Panama City only to find that the hotel is overbooked and there's no room for you. Or, you're stranded in Mexico for three days because your flight's been mysteriously delayed. The best way to avoid getting burned by a tour company is to check it out carefully. Talk to friends who've gone on spring break through the company you're considering. What kind of experience did they have?

Also, find out if the tour company belongs to major industry groups like the American Society of Travel Agents (ASTA), the National Tour Operators Association (NTA) or the International Airlines Travel Agent Network. (IATAN). If it doesn't belong to at least one of these organizations, think twice before booking your trip. To find out if any formal complaints have been lodged against a tour operator, contact the Better Business Bureau in the operator's home city or the attorney general's office in the operator's home state.

Don't be afraid to go on your own personal fact-finding mission to verify a tour operator's claims. If the friendly sales agent promises that you will stay at the Ocean Princess Beach Resort in Cancún, call the Ocean Princess and find out if the tour operator does indeed have rooms booked there, and how many. Unfortunately, it's not uncommon for tour companies to exaggerate. Students, of course, don't discover the truth until they're on vacation, at which point they're still at the mercy of the company. Even if compensation comes later, which it rarely does, it doesn't make up for a disappointing vacation.

Finally, get a feel for the company's financial stability. By law, tour operators must keep the money you paid for your trip in an escrow account until you actually travel. Ask the tour operator which bank keeps this account. Then call the bank to make sure the account exists. If the company is reluctant to tell you where the account is, or if you find out there is no account, cut out immediately.

The Thing About Chartered Flights

If it weren't for charter airlines, students would pay exorbitant prices to fly south for spring break. This is because March is prime migration season for northern snow birds fed up with sallow skin and Seasonal Affective Disorder. They are the ones who book up every last south-bound commercial flight months in advance. To bring the scales of supply and demand back into balance, tour operators simply hire charter airlines to ferry travelers to the tropics.

It's important to know that charter airlines don't run the way commercial airlines do. First of all, the Department of Transportation dictates charter plane schedules, and usually releases this information to tour operators only a few weeks ahead of time. Since tour operators will not know the flight schedule when you make your trip reservations, they will give you a three-day window within which you'll depart. Usually, Friday, Saturday or Sunday. You'll find out the exact date and time shortly before your trip.

While charter airlines make spring break travel financially feasible for students, they are not as big or dependable as commercial carriers. A number of students found this out the hard way on spring break '97. On March 7, the Federal Aviation Administration grounded AV Atlantic Airlines, which had contracted with one big tour company to take thousands of spring breakers to Cancún, Mazatlán and Nassau. Most spring breakers eventually got where they were going, but not without experiencing delays, inconvenience and confusion. AV Atlantic subsequently declared bankruptcy.

The best way to avoid this kind of fiasco is to find out which charter company your prospective tour operator is using. Then check the company's track record by calling the Federal Aviation Administration (FAA) or the U.S. Department of Transportation at 202-366-4000.

A Short List of Tour Operators

Below are just a few of the many tour companies that offer spring break trips to the beach. Remember, price estimates, are just that. Always call to get the most up-to-date rates.

Breakaway Tours

Toronto, Canada
1-800-465-4257
http://www.breakawaytours.com
Domestic destinations: .... Daytona Beach, Panama City
Low-end price estimate
    for bus and hotel: .... $199-$249
International destinations: .... None
Free trips: .... 1 for every 20 sign-ups.

Inter-Campus Programs

West Chicago, IL
1-800-327-6013
http://www.icpt.com
Domestic destinations: .... Daytona Beach, Panama City,
                                            Key West, South Padre Island

**Low-end price estimate
   for bus and hotel:** $225
International destinations: ...... Cancún, Mexico; Nassau, Bahamas, Montego Bay and Negril, Jamaica
**Low-end price estimate
   for airfare and hotel:** $399
All-inclusive packages: .... Yes
Free trips: .... 1 for every 20 sign-ups

Student Travel Services

Hanover, MD
1-800-648-4849
http://www.ststravel.com
Domestic destinations: .... Daytona Beach, Panama City
**Low-end price estimate
   for bus and hotel:** $210
International destinations: ...... Cancún, Mexico; Montego Bay and Negril, Jamaica
**Low-end price estimate
   for airfare and hotel:** $429
All-inclusive trips: .... Yes
Free trips: .... 1 for every 15 sign-ups.

Take A Break Student Travel

Boston, MA
1-800-328-7283
http://www.takeabreak.com/
Domestic destinations: .... Daytona Beach, Panama City
**Low-end price estimate
   hotel only:** $140
International destinations: ...... Cancún and Mazátlan, Mexico; Nassau, Bahamas
**Low-end price estimate
   for airfare and hotel:** $400
All-inclusive trips: .... Yes
Free trips: .... 1 for every 15 sign-ups.

Sun Splash Tours

New York, NY
1-800-426-7710
http://www.sunsplashtours.com
Domestic destinations: .... Daytona Beach, Panama City,
South Padre Island
**Low-end price estimate
for bus and hotel:** $209
International destinations: ...... Cancún, Mexico; Nassau, Bahamas;
Montego Bay and Negril, Jamaica
**Low-end price estimate
for airfare and hotel:** $400
All-inclusive trips: .... Yes
Free trips: .... 1 for every 15 sign-ups.

Sunchase Tours

Fort Collins, CO
1-800-786-2427
http://www.sunchase.com
Domestic destinations: .... Daytona Beach, Panama City,
South Padre Island, Key West,
Hilton Head, SC
**Low-end price estimate
for hotel only:** $130
International destinations: ...... None
All-inclusive trips: .... None
Free trips: .... 1 for every 15 sign-ups.

Vagabond Tours

New Brunswick, NJ
1-800-678-6386
http://vagabondtours.com
Domestic destinations: .... Daytona Beach, Panama City
**Low-end price estimate
for bus and hotel:** $209
International Destinations: ..... Cancún, Mexico; Nassau, Bahamas

Low-end price estimates
    for airfare and hotel: $379
All-inclusive trips: ....Yes
Free trips: ....1 for every 15 sign-ups.

Have Some Free Stuff

Spring break certainly engenders some major contradictions. For example, while you'll pay big bucks to get into bars or secure a room, you'll find that free samples and souvenirs rain down endlessly. This is because, you, spring breakers, have done the corporate world a big favor. You've gathered together a substantial portion of your demographic group in one place. What could make marketing easier? And market they do, from underneath awnings at the beach, in front of clubs and in hotel lobbies. Wherever you go, the corporate world is weaving its web (or, in advertising-speak, "developing a relationship with the consumer") with free stuff you can't resist. T-shirts, watches, duffel bags, sunscreen, lip balm, beer cups, pool floats, granola bars, candy bars, chewing gum, soft drinks, toothpaste, perfume, cologne, key chains, condoms, condom key chains, frisbees, visors and lighters.

Tough Breaks

In 1996, 20-year-old University of Albany student, Peter Schlendorf popped a few too many ULTIMATE Xphoria pills while he was partying in Florida. Little did he know, the over-the-counter stimulant, which mimics the effects of the illegal drug Ecstasy, would kill him. No doubt, 24-year old Carter Gray of Kentucky, was equally unaware of his fate when he ventured down to Panama City for spring break last March. The good times ended early when he fell from his fourth floor hotel balcony during a drinking binge. He suffered a fractured skull, broken ribs, collapsed lungs, a broken leg and abdominal injuries, barely escaping with his life.

Schlendorf and Gray became two more of spring break's unwitting victims: Students who said, "Nope, it won't happen to me!," but were all too sadly mistaken. The fact is, spring breakers do not generally get hurt in freak accidents. They get hurt because they or their friends abuse drugs and alcohol. Whether, it's drunk driving, alcohol poisoning, alcohol-related accidents or drug-induced seizures, in most cases, it's entirely preventable.

Drunk Driving

Being the hard-drinking fiesta it is, spring break is a prime breeding ground for drunk drivers. It may start innocently enough. You're prepared to stop after a few drinks, but then you start enjoying yourself so you flick the scolding angel off your shoulder and knock back a few more. Or maybe you didn't realize that only three drinks would affect you so much? Or maybe, you assumed that since you drove to the bar, one of your friends would drive back, leaving you free to swill.

Whatever the situation, when it's time to head home, machismo or simple bad judgment take over and you, or one of your not-so-sober friends, get behind the wheel. Here's hoping you get pulled

over before you end up twisted around a tree or in jail for man-
slaughter. Although awareness about drunk driving has increased
over the last fifteen years, it still happens, and is, in fact, the leading
cause of death for 15 to 24 year-olds in the United States.

Blood Alcohol Concentration (BAC)

In Florida, a Blood Alcohol Concentration (BAC) of .08% will get
you arrested for drunk driving. If you're under 21, the limit drops
to just .02%. In Texas, BAC limits are .1% for those 21 and over, and
.07% for the under-21 set. If you are caught driving drunk, you
could face a hefty fine and the revocation of your license. And that,
of course, is only if you don't hurt anyone.

So how many drinks does it take to get to these BAC levels? Well,
it depends on your weight and the period of time over which you
consume the drinks. After consuming four standard size drinks (a
12-ounce beer or a 1.5-ounce shot) in two hours, a 120 pound student will have a BAC of about .09%. Under the same conditions, a
140 pound student will have a BAC of about .08% and a 160 pound
student will have a BAC of about .06%.

The absorption of alcohol into your bloodstream will be slower
if you have food in your stomach or if you are drinking juice-based
mixed drinks. Absorption will speed up if you are drinking mixed
drinks made with carbonated beverages. Eventually, no matter how
much you've eaten or how you've mixed your drinks, all the alcohol you've consumed will end up in your bloodstream.

Designated Drivers

Hear Mom's voice echo in your brain: "Do you have a designated
driver driver driver? Be sure to take your *turn turn turn*! Remember,
Mother's Day is next *month month month*!" Pick your designated
driver before you hit the bars each night and give that person the
car keys before the drinking starts. If, for some reason, your designated driver wusses out and you're left with Smashed, Blitzed or
Bombed as your chauffeur, don't hesitate to call a cab. Your life is
worth the extra ten bucks.

Free Rides, No Proselytizing

If you're in Panama City, Daytona Beach, Key West or Lake Havasu, you can get a free ride back to your hotel between 8 p.m. and 3 a.m. courtesy of Beach Reach, an initiative sponsored by the Southern Baptist Convention. Student volunteers hand out cards bearing the Beach Reach ride number at the beach and outside popular spring break clubs. If you don't have the number, local police or club security should know where to find it.

Beach Reach also provides free pancake breakfasts between 9 a.m. and noon daily for spring breakers. These friendly, well-attended breakfasts are usually set up in local parking lots by Beach Reach students and other volunteers. The same folks sponsor Beach Express Coffeehouses where students can get dessert and coffee and hear live bands from 8 p.m. to 1 a.m. each night. Again, the event is free.

Bacchus and Gamma

You'll probably see these names if you head to Panama City or South Padre Island, and you'll probably wonder who they are. Wonder no more! These twin organizations strive to promote safe alcohol consumption among college students. This is not to say they're a couple of teetotalers clubs looking to launch the next Prohibition. In fact, just to get this point across, Bacchus (Boosting Alcohol Consciousness Concerning the Health of University Students) borrowed its name from the Greek god of wine. Gamma (Greeks Advocating Mature Management of Alcohol) furthers the same message with fraternities and sororities.

Together, these groups sponsor an annual "Safe Spring Break" campaign which focuses on drunk driving prevention. If there is a Bacchus or Gamma chapter at your school, it will probably hold a pledge card drive shortly before spring break. Go ahead, sign up! All you have to do is promise not to drink and drive while you're on break. You could be the lucky pledge card-signer who wins the wheels. In 1997, you would have had your choice between a Jeep Wrangler and a Plymouth Neon.

At the beach (Panama City or Padre Island), Bacchus and Gamma sponsor a number of fun activities they hope will tear students away from their beer coolers long enough to give them "natural" highs. Highlights include rock-climbing, parasailing, tug of wars, ersatz sumo wrestling, bungee running, velcro wall-jumping (à la David Letterman) and basketball and volleyball tournaments.

If you would like to find out more about Bacchus and Gamma or start a chapter on your campus, contact:

The Bacchus and Gamma Peer Education Network
P.O. Box 100430
Denver, CO 80250-0430
(303) 871-0901
e-mail: bacgam@aol.com
web: http://bacchusgamma.org

Alcohol Poisoning

Alcohol poisoning is dangerous because it can be hard to detect. When your friend's tossed back quite a few drinks and is passed out on the floor, it's tempting to let him sleep. This, however, may be the worst thing you can do. If there is too much alcohol in his brain, his sleep center may become "depressed" and he may stop breathing. If you suspect alcohol poisoning, first, try to rouse him. If he responds, but is listless and drowsy, turn him on his side so he won't choke if he vomits. If you can't wake him up, but he is breathing regularly, check his breathing every few minutes. If his breathing is irregular, call 911 or notify authorities immediately. If he stops breathing, start mouth-to-mouth resuscitation.

Roofies

Female college students should be especially wary of roofies, brand name Rohypnol, when they go on spring break. Ten times stronger than Valium, it is also known as the "date rape" drug. The scenario plays out like this: A stranger dissolves the tasteless, odorless white tablet in an unsuspecting woman's drink. About ten minutes later, the woman begins to feel dizzy and disoriented. She may have difficulty moving or speaking and will eventually pass out. The stranger rapes her while she is unconscious. When she wakes up, she has no memory of what happened, nor of the person who gave her the doctored drink.

The best way to protect yourself against this kind of episode is to keep an eye on your drink at all times. If some Romeo offers to buy a round, let him, but accompany him to the bar. Once you've got your drink in hand, keep it there until you're ready to get rid of it. If you leave it on a table or bar while you dance, consider it history. You're better off spending a couple dollars on a new drink than slurping up a tainted one.

Just last March, in time for spring break '97, the Florida State legislature stiffened the penalty for using or selling roofies, placing it in the same legal category as heroin and LSD. Previously, it was classified with such low-abuse drugs as Valium.

Dealing With Rape

If you are the victim of rape, whether you were under the influence of Roofies, alcohol or nothing at all, don't be afraid to report it. No one has the right to force you to have sex. Get a friend to act as your advocate. Tell her what happened and ask her to accompany you when you talk to the police.

Many sexual assault victims feel angry and confused about what happened to them, and want to talk to someone, but don't know where to turn. A trained counselor at a rape crisis hotline may be able to help. If you are on spring break and can't find the local hotline number, call the Rape, Assault and Incest National Network (RAINN) at **1-800-656-HOPE**. Based in Washington, DC, this national hotline operates 24 hours a day, seven days a week. When you call the hotline, a computer will read your current area code and the first three digits of the phone number, then instantly reroute the call to the nearest crisis center. If the line is busy, the call will be routed to the next closest crisis center. All costs are paid by RAINN.

Liquid X (GHB)

Also known as Liquid Ecstasy or Liquid E, Gamma Hydroxy Butyrate (GHB) has become popular in the underground club and rave scene as an alternative to ecstasy or speed. It is a salty-tasting, colorless liquid that usually comes in a small plastic bottle. One dose is usually a capful, though it can vary widely since GHB is often manufactured on stovetops in home "laboratories." Like alcohol, GHB relaxes users and decreases their social inhibitions. At high doses, users can become so heavily sedated they feel helpless and immobile. Some users also have seizures. GBH can be lethal when taken with alcohol or tranquilizers, causing respiratory collapse or coma.

Although, European pharmaceutical companies do manufacture GHB (in powdered form), the kind most often sold in American clubs is homemade. Thus, its potency is likely to vary from batch to batch, making its effects on users unpredictable. There is also no telling what impurities are present in homemade versions of the drug. In Florida, GHB resides in the same legal class as morphine, one step below heroin.

Uncle Sam vs. the Chemically-Enhanced Student

Besides ravaging your body, drugs can quickly derail your college dreams. You see, Uncle Sam gets very testy when he finds out that his federal student aid recipients are using drugs. In fact, he gets so burnt up about it that he'll cancel a student's Pell Grant, Stafford Loan, or Perkins Loan immediately, if there's a conviction for drug possession or distribution. Let this be a warning to all of you who are normally level-headed and responsible, and wouldn't dare touch the stuff.

Sex on the Beach

Your starry eyes meet across the dance floor and you know at that moment you were made for each other. Yeah right! Maybe in a Brothers Grimm tale. Now for the Reality Bites version of your spring break fling. You wake up with a pounding headache and a stranger in your bed hogging the blanket. It's a great morning. Did you use a condom? Did you use any protection at all? You have no idea.

No doubt about it, sex happens on spring break. What's unfortunate, is that it often happens when both parties have had too much to drink and aren't thinking straight. It's usually well after the beaches have cleared and students have gone back to class that negative consequences, such as sexually transmitted diseases or unwanted pregnancies, manifest themselves. The moral of the story: Don't let yourself get so out of control that you don't remember, or can't manage, to use a condom or some other form of protection when you have sex on spring break.

The Fake ID Blues

The bouncer eyes your driver's license suspiciously and asks you your birth date. You rattle it off like a pro, "January 17, 1973." He shoots back, "When did you graduate from high school?" You're caught off guard, "ummm, ahhh, um, in 1996," you answer honestly. "Funny," he points out, "how last year you were a fresh-faced 18-year old and now you're a jaded 24-year old. "That *is* funny," you stammer as your fake ID disappears into his pocket and you get yanked aside by the manager.

Bars and clubs popular with the spring break crowd know about half of their patrons will not be 21. They also know they could lose their liquor licenses if they serve this segment of their clientele. Thus, most spring break bars and clubs proof hard. Some even bring in hard-core ID-checkers from other cities for the spring break season. Fake IDs rarely fly with these bouncers. They know what to look for and what to ask. Where you see a face practically indistinguishable from your own, they'll see your older sister or brother. If you get caught using a fake ID, count on it being taken away. What happens next depends on the club. Some may simply bar you from entering even with an under-21 stamp. Others may turn you over to the local police, who will probably give you a lecture and a fine.

In the worst case scenario, you'll have tested your luck in Key West, Florida. Here, breakers who try to use fake or altered IDs get to go to Spring Break Court. In this five-year old institution, which convenes at 8 a.m. seven days a week through spring break season, students are given a choice between a $175 dollar fine and eight hours of community service. Most opt for the latter, which means picking up litter, pulling weeds or painting government buildings for a day. To top it off, each member of the "spring break chain gang" wears a bright orange shirt with the words *Monroe County Jail* emblazoned on the back.

Bacon on the Beach

Attention all you milky-white breakers! Take precautions when you tan. If you're determined to get some color, do so gradually. Remember, you don't have to become the Coppertone model within your first six hours at the beach. You have an entire lazy week to accomplish the transformation. Not only will it be less painful, it will be healthier in the long run. For one thing, you'll reduce your chances of getting skin cancer, which strikes one in seven Americans. Too many students rebuff the warnings saying, "Life is short!" To them we say, "Exactly. Why make it shorter?"

The bottom line is this: Don't brave the rays, especially between 10 a.m. and 2 p.m., without applying sun block of at least 15 SPF. You may want to put an even higher SPF on your face, which is most susceptible to wrinkles and melanoma later on. Even when it's overcast, you should not go without sun protection. The sun's harmful rays have never been deterred by a few clouds. As you get a little color, which is your natural shield against the sun, you can gradually work your way down to a lower SPF. The worst thing the light-skinned crowd can do is slather on burn-accelerating tanning oils. Chances are, you'll get a nasty, blistering burn this way, which, besides looking awful, will hurt a good sight, too.

Domestic Destinations

FOUR

PANAMA CITY BEACH

MTV has made this Gulf Coast city its spring break head-quarters for the last two years, setting off a hedonistic frenzy among college students each March. But the "Redneck Riviera" is not without its native charms. White sand beaches and two Byzantine night clubs make Panama City Beach a natural choice for party-starved college students. Also, because it lies in the northern part of the state, it means shorter drives for locationally-challenged spring breakers. By the same token, its temperature is typically a few degrees cooler than in Daytona or Fort Lauderdale. While fine for sun-bathing, it's mostly too cold for a for a full-fledged ocean plunge.

72°
Avg March
HIGH

Like any low-budget resort area, Panama City has its share of beach sprawl. T-shirt shops, tattoo parlors, fast-food restaurants and amusements dominate the main beach-side strip. If you've always felt there just wasn't enough breakfast food in the world, this is the town for you. Waffle Houses, Omelette Houses and Pancake Houses abound.

A Scene From the Beach

A gaggle of breakers bury one of their friends in the sand up to his neck. Close by, a weathered local shucks raw oysters, squirts them with lemon and tosses them down with a chaser from his silver flask. He makes friendly conversation with passing students. Spying the sand-covered young man, he heads over and offers him an oyster. The student declines, looking somewhat repulsed by the prospect. The local decides that horizons must be broadened and goes ahead and readies the oyster. As a crowd gathers around the spectacle, the student's friends break out their cameras. The local brings the oyster, spritzed with lemon, to the squirming student's mouth. With no hands free to rebuff the offering, the student has no choice but to suck it down. He does so with a grimace. As onlookers cheer, the student musters a half smile. The local gives him a swig from the silver flask for his efforts.

Nightlife in Panama City Beach

Next door neighbors Club La Vela and Spinnaker, form the cosmic center of the Panama City Beach nightlife. If you've spent the last six months hanging out in hole-in-the-wall college bars, these multiplexes of clubdom will give you culture shock. Not surprisingly, most students make the transition. Thousands (literally) cram into La Vela and Spinnaker every night during the height of spring break season. The best thing about these clubs is that with so many different rooms and stages, there really is something for everyone. You can just as easily groove to techno as you can jam to vintage 80's tunes or watch a cover band playing Live and Bush.

Be prepared to pay for all this fun. Cover prices usually start around $10 early in the night and can climb as high as $25 if the clubs get crowded. Drinks, of course, will cost you too, even water. You can beat the gouging if you arrive early in the evening, by about 7 or 8 p.m. Typically, there's no cover then, plus there's a good chance you'll get free drinks.

Daily Doin's

During the day, when entrance is free, Spinnaker and La Vela remain the hub of beach front activity. The decks are a good place to seek shade, rehydrate and listen to some tunes. If you're not fond of ocean swimming, take a dip in their deckside pools. If you're lucky (it helps if MTV is in town), you might hear big name bands like Aerosmith, Collective Soul or No Doubt warm up for night time concerts on the clubs' outdoor stages.

Of course, the requisite wet t-shirt, hot male body and other flesh-revealing contests occur regularly at Spinnaker and La Vela. But breakers hardly need to venture into the clubs for a show. The beach might as well be one giant runway, a showcase for the tanned and toned in all their scantily clad glory. This is not to say that there aren't plenty of regular people on the beach, just that the ones aspiring to careers on the catwalk are more noticeable.

Spring Break Stories: Thanks MTV!

I spent spring break '97 in Panama City during MTV's Spring Break Week. Although I was never a big fan of MTV's game show "Singled Out," I was coerced into being part of the studio audience by my friend Amy. My duties as an official member of the studio audience included standing around on the deck of a massive club, clapping, screaming and looking extremely happy and enthusiastic. A potential reward was being caught by a camera that occasionally panned over the crowd.

Anyway, after back-to-back tapings, I needed to use the bathroom in order to survive the third and final taping. My first attempts to get to one inside the club were foiled because security people were keeping the throngs of students out of large areas of the club reserved for the use of MTV crews and "Singled Out" contestants. What I would've given for a shiny pink "Singled Out" contestant sticker!

Finally, I found a bathroom that was unguarded. I left the bathroom through its back entrance and found myself in a club lounge in the company of the official contestants from "Singled Out," as well as a catered buffet lunch. I congratulated myself on outwitting MTV's extensive security forces. Although I wore neither a skimpy bikini nor multiple ID badges, I decided to help myself to lunch. My turkey sub and bottled water, courtesy MTV, made my day. On the way out, I snagged an official "Singled Out" t-shirt for Amy. My single regret was that I hadn't found this entrance the day before when Stone Temple Pilots had been in the club.

Claire Sayles '97
SUNY Binghamton
Binghamton, NY

Who Partakes

The spring break crowd at Panama City Beach is not exactly what you'd call diverse. Most breakers are white, with students of any color scarce. The standard age range is 18-24, though there's sure to be a few high-schoolers and a few thirty-somethings in the mix. The male-female ratio is somewhat skewed, about 3 or 4 to one.

Alcohol Policy

Florida state law prohibits open alcohol containers on public property (which includes the beach). Then again, a law doesn't mean much if it's not enforced, which is the case in Panama City during spring break. When the Panama City Beach Convention and Visitors

Bureau states, "You can party on the beach and the local constabu-
lary will not hassle you," they aren't kidding. Open alcohol containers abound, and many students drink with abandon. Police do patrol the area, but are not generally concerned with the legion of
drinking youth. That said, they will confront imbibers who look particularly young, as if maybe they're still working on a high school
diploma.

Getting Around

Here's hoping you drive to Panama City, because if you don't, you're
in for a major headache. Things are spread out here and there's no
public transportation to speak of. Front Beach Road is the town's
main drag, but the nightclubs La Vela and Spinnaker reside a good
distance away on Thomas Drive. Even for the hardiest health nut,
walking around Panama City is a pipe dream.

DRIVING DISTANCES	
Atlanta, GA	287 Miles
Boston, MA	1308
Columbus, OH	842
Detroit, MI	975
Nashville, TN	476
New York, NY	1112
Orlando, FL	340
Philadelphia, PA	1068
Pittsburgh, PA	973
St. Louis, MO	745
Washington, DC	922

PANAMA CITY

PANAMA CITY BEACH WEB RESOURCES

Panama City Beach

http://interoz.com/pcb
This is the more "official" of the two sites, and includes a calendar
of events, maps, weather links and local phone numbers.

Welcome to Panama City Beach

http://www.travelfile.com/get?pcbeach

Sponsored by the Panama City Convention and Visitors Bureau, this site has contains all the basics from driving times to nightlife picks.

DAYTONA BEACH

75°

Avg March HIGH

If spring break in Panama City is about MTV glitter, spring break in Daytona is about chrome. Exhibit 1: The Daytona International Speedway. This local showpiece plays host to some of the biggest car and motorcycle races in the country. And, since spring break comes on the heels of Bike Week, there are always a few bikers in town when the swim suit set arrives. Early bird breakers who get to town in time for Bike Week's Sunday finale, are in for a special treat, as on this day 100,000 hogs (derived from Harley Owner's Group) gather for the "Blessing of the Bikes" before parading to the Speedway for the Daytona 200.

Even when the race cars and bikes are mostly in repose, it's easy to see that motor vehicles are revered in Daytona. Auto enthusiasts deck their cars out with flashy, designer hub caps and custom color paint jobs and soup them up with lifters and the like. Given the machine mania in Daytona, it should come as no surprise that cars are permitted on the beach. (Motorists must pay a $5 fee and enter on designated ramps.) Cruising is a popular activity, and during prime sun hours, there's always a line of cars rolling along the beach. Many breakers simply drive on and park, infusing Daytona's beach scene with something of a tailgate party atmosphere, though it's a little more subdued than your average pre-football bash. How rowdy can it get when many of the participants are lying on the sand dozing?

Daytona's Big Turnaround

MTV started coming to Daytona in 1986. For eight years, the network brought shows, bands and celebs to town for the annual bacchanal, attracting the hardest of hard-core: the sloppiest drunks, the lewdest exhibitionists, and the most destructive lodgers. By 1993, the city's merchants and hotel owners were fed up. In June, they voted to cut off all tax-payer funded spring break promotions. That December, MTV announced it would take its spring break party to San Diego. Thus, the scene was set for Daytona's spring break makeover.

To keep the college students in and the mayhem out, city officials set about putting some structure into spring break. They brought in big corporate-sponsored activity venues like the Sports Illustrated Beach Club, the Gatorade Spring Break Village and the NBA Jam Van. Today's breakers can still drink themselves into oblivion, but they can also take part in volleyball tournaments, basketball games, obstacle courses, rollerblade derbies, gladiator jousting matches or sand-sculpting contests.

Wanna Job?

In Daytona, you'll be able to walk into a job interview in a bikini or trunks without receiving an instant dismissal. In fact, in all likelihood, your interviewer will be dressed casually too. It's all part of a career fair that caters to spring breakers. Begun in 1995, as part of Daytona's drive to clean up spring break, the two-day fair gives students a chance to chat with prospective employers. Participants fill out a "mini-resume" and are then matched up with interested recruiters. You won't get hired on the spot, but if you pique a recruiter's interest, you may very well land a second interview. In 1997, 30 companies, including AT&T, Arthur Anderson, Eddie Bauer, Lucent Technologies, the Peace Corps and the United States Secret Service, attended the fair.

Spring Break Stories: Greg Louganis He's Not

We arrive at the Holiday Inn Sunspree pool in the middle of a belly flop-off. It's down to two contenders, both remarkably similar in appearance. Frat boys: roly-poly and dough faced, hamming it up like there's no tomorrow. One after another they go flying off the board, which is about 10 feet above the pool. You can't help but feel vicarious tingles of pain as they slap down onto the water. Since crowd noise is the deciding factor, there is complete pandemonium on the pool deck. It's clear that each respective fraternity clan is doing everything in their power to see that their brother becomes belly flop champion.

Eventually, the DJ awards the title to one of them and announces another contest: A pairs race, the catch is that the female half of the pair must be sitting on a very flimsy inner tube float pushed by the male half of the pair. In a second, everybody is running around the deck in search of a partner. It takes only a little prodding to get my friend Kelly off and running to find a fellow. Before long, she's lined herself up a boy named Bash. We know that's his name because it's tattooed on his chest. Appropriately, he looks like a linebacker.

The whistle blows and the race is on. Half of the float-riders capsize before they're even half way across the pool. By the third lap, it looks like Kelly and Bash have it wrapped up. But then at the last moment, Kelly flails and takes a dunk, joining most of the other racers who are log-jammed in the middle of the pool. Even though Kelly looks like a wet rat when she surfaces, she hops back on the float and she and Bash make one last ditch effort. Despite their valiant attempt, they lose to a pair whose float-rider looks like Barbie.

Laura Blackburn '98
University of North Carolina
Chapel Hill, NC

Nightlife in Daytona Beach

The Baja Beach Club and Razzles are the two major stops in Daytona's nightlife circuit, at least for spring breakers. Compared to Panama City's Spinnaker and La Vela, they are down-home joints, with pool tables and video games in the same rooms as their dance floors. Still, breakers are no less crazy, and maybe even a little more so, what with test-tube shooters available at every turn and bar-top dancing alive and well. Even if MTV isn't officially in town, there's a good chance that Singled Out will go on location at one of these clubs. Covers average around $10.

Although Daytona is not where most people would expect to find a hip, eclectic coffee house, JavaLava, located just a stone's throw from Baja and Razzles, fits the bill. The perfect pre- or post-club hang-out, in addition to a couple dozen different coffee drinks, it offers a full selection of alcoholic beverages, from microbrew to hot saké.

Who Partakes

Like Panama City, Daytona attracts a mostly white, 18-24 crowd, from the southern and eastern states. Canadian students are also in the mix during the early part of the spring break season, so much so that enterprising city officials have dubbed the last week in February and the first week in March "Canadian Fun Weeks."

"Black College Reunion" weekend caps Daytona's spring break season in early April. The event, which began in 1984, grew out of a football rivalry between Bethune-Cookman College and Florida A&M University. Today, the event attracts over 75,000 students from 115 Historically Black Colleges and Universities.

Alcohol Policy

Drinking is not permitted on Daytona's beaches. Signs are posted and the police enforce the law. That said, the beach is big and chaotic, and some breakers discreetly bend the rules.

Getting Around

Daytona Beach is separated from the mainland by the Halifax River. Local buses run between the two, though not at night or on Sundays. Beachside, trolley service is available along the central part of Atlantic Avenue (Highway A1A), Daytona's main strip, from noon until midnight. The fare for both bus and trolley is 75 cents.

DRIVING DISTANCES	
Atlanta, GA	435 Miles
Boston, MA	1275
Columbus, OH	909
Detroit, MI	1151
Nashville, TN	681
New York, NY	1044
Orlando, FL	56
Philadelphia	957
Pittsburgh, PA	913
St. Louis, MO	988
Washington, DC	810

DAYTONA BEACH

DAYTONA BEACH WEB RESOURCES

Daytona Beach Spring Break
http://www.1idea.com/daytonabreak/
Sponsored by Daytona's Convention and Visitors Bureau, this site has the dirt on the town's spring break festivities as well as basic travel and hotel information.

Spring Break Photo Essay
http://www.journale.com/SPRBREAK/springbreakintro.html
Against all odds, photographer W. Keith McManus managed to transform spring break into something kind of artsy. His black and white photos capture the essence of spring break in Daytona during the late eighties

FORT LAUDERDALE

80°

Avg March HIGH

Once the mightiest of spring break cities, Fort Lauderdale was sent to detox in 1985 by mayor Bob Cox. He enacted laws prohibiting drinking outdoors, camping on the beach and overnight parking, and ordered strict enforcement of hotel and club occupancy laws. To drive the point home, he went on national TV telling breakers to stay away. The mayor's strategy worked. Out went the wet t-shirt and banana eating contests and in came a gentrified family-friendly resort. Today, horror stories about 350,000 drink-waving, traffic-snarling breakers are the stuff of long-ago news briefs.

The big question? Can spring breakers set foot on Fort Lauderdale's sands without getting run out of town on a rail? And if so, is there any hope of having fun? The answer to the first is a definitive yes. Fort Lauderdale no longer has a fight to pick with students now that things have been cleaned up. As for fun, sure, unless it involves beer-funneling and balcony-scaling. In other words, if you are looking for the "real" spring break experience, you'd better go to Panama City or Daytona. If, however, you want to sit back and relax in true beach fashion, Fort Lauderdale will suit you just fine. (The original spring breakers of the 1960s didn't come here for nothing.)

The Current Scene

One benefit of Fort Lauderdale's transformation is that its beaches have improved and the city has become decidedly cosmopolitan. A park-like atmosphere pervades the beach. There are grills, picnic tables, jungle gyms and even the occasional hammock. While the main beach strip (along Route A1A) is well-peopled, it's certainly not towel-to-towel like in Panama City. Bordering the beach is a pedestrian promenade popular with rollerbladers and cyclists. The south side of the beach outside the Sheraton Yankee Trader Hotel is a volleyballer's mecca with pick-up games on dozens of courts. Across A1A, breakers and vacationers linger in outdoor cafes and bars. On Las Olas, which runs straight to the beach, specialty boutiques and chi-chi eateries rule the day.

One drawback to Fort Lauderdale's renaissance is that prices have gone up. It's not as easy as it used to be to live on chili dogs and cheap beer for a week. Nor is it a snap to find a divey hotel that tolerates the old ten-to-a-room ratio.

Nightlife in Lauderdale

Once upon a time, the Candy Store, the Button Club and the Elbo Room were Fort Lauderdale's premier spring break watering holes. Today, only the Elbo Room remains, but it's still going strong at the corner of Las Olas and A1A. While certainly a monument to spring break past, it's moved into the future with remarkable ease. Its newest addition? The Elbo Cam, a video camera mounted on top of the bar, which beams scenes from the pub and the surrounding beach onto the World Wide Web. (http://www.justsurfit.com/elboroom/cam1.shtml)

While always a lively joint, the Elbo Room is relatively small and can get old rather quickly. Instead of settling in for the night, pencil it into your bar crawl. You might also hit the Baja Beach Club, which offers the standard spring break fare. If you're looking for an alternative club, check out The Edge or Squeeze. For variety, Trios is a good bet, featuring (surprise!) 3 clubs in one.

Who Partakes

Many of Ft. Lauderdale's spring breakers are Florida students who live only a few hours away. It is also a popular destination for singles in their late-twenties and early-thirties who want to have a good time, but can't go full-throttle the way 18-year olds can. And of course, breakers will share the beach with a good number of families.

Alcohol Policy

Alcohol and glass bottles are prohibited on Lauderdale's beaches, as many prominently posted signs indicate. It's not police patrols or lifeguards that enforces the prohibition though. Instead, ye old Honor Code keeps the beaches dry.

Getting Around

A car is handy in Fort Lauderdale, but not necessary as the city's public transportation is well-developed and accessible. The Wave Line Trolley runs along the main part of the lengthy beach strip (Route A1A) and the local buses service runs regularly between downtown Lauderdale and the beach.

DRIVING DISTANCES	
Atlanta, GA	643 Miles
Boston, MA	1509
Columbus, OH	1143
Detroit, MI	1382
Nashville, TN	888
New York, NY	1285
Orlando, FL	213
Philadelphia	1191
Pittsburgh, PA	1148
St. Louis, MO	1195
Washington, DC	1045

FT. LAUDERDALE

FORT LAUDERDALE WEB RESOURCES

The City of Fort Lauderdale Online
http://info.ci.ftlaud.fl.us/
This is Fort Lauderdale's official web site. It contains some useful tourist tidbits along with a heap of local-oriented information.

Greater Fort Lauderdale Convention and Visitors Bureau
http://www.co.broward.fl.us/sunny.htm
This site contains Fort Lauderdale's official events calendar, as well as a listing of hotels, restaurants, bars and clubs.

KEY WEST

79°

Avg March
HIGH

Spring breakers can't help but love what is perhaps Key West's most illuminating nickname: Margaritaville. (Those who drive down will also come to appreciate another unofficial moniker: Southernmost City.) Coined by singer Jimmy Buffet, the name describes Key West's collective state of mind as well as one of its favorite beverages. Students gladly adopt both as their own, often traveling thousands of miles to do so.

The beaches are brief in Key West, but otherwise it's got all the trappings of spring break: warm 'n sunny weather; bars and liquor stores galore; and, of course, hoards of college students. About 45,000 breakers journey down to this Gulf of Mexico Island every March. Although tourism is certainly the fuel that powers Key West, it isn't the strip-mall variety that pervades spring break towns like Panama City or Daytona Beach. Quirky and kitschy is more the rule.

Nightlife in Key West

First of all, breakers shouldn't miss Key West's famous Technicolor sunsets, nor the nightly entertainment that accompanies them on Mallory Docks. Among the jugglers and street musicians is always the odd stunt man who can balance a fully loaded shopping cart on his teeth. Once the sun's down and it's time to get on with the night's business, stroll along Duval Street in the Old Town quarter. It houses some of the hottest spring break haunts, including Sloppy Joe's, Rick's Rum Runners and Dirty Harry's. If you're not drawn in by their claims to have hosted literary legend Ernest Hemingway, maybe the live music and $10 all-you-can-drink deals will get you.

Spring Break Stories: Wanted—A Good Night's Sleep In Key West

Camping is most definitely illegal within the city limits—and that law is seriously enforced! Particularly free camping, that is, just picking an unobtrusive spot and pitching your tent overnight. My friend Avi and I tried camping under some trees behind a residential trailer park our first night in Key West, since the legit campgrounds were too expensive (we were nearly broke) and way out of town. We were woken up at 7 a.m. by a guy walking his dog, who casually informed us that his neighbor had called the cops on us. Before we could take the tent down, a squad car pulled up and two cops swaggered over to our site.

They asked us for our ID, and one of them quizzed us while we took down the tent. The other cop called headquarters and gave them our descriptions, and then walked up to me and asked, "When did you leave Orlando?" and a lot of other questions like he thought I was some escaped felon! As if a criminal would go on the lam with a bicycle!

So things went from bad to worse. As soon as the tent was packed up, they said that we were going to be charged with violating the no-camping law and we were going down to the station with them. However, before I could ask them what we were going to do with our bikes, their car radio starting blasting an APB about a break-in at a bank, and they piled into their car in a hurry, pausing just long enough to say, "If we catch you doing this again, you're in deep sh—!" If some guy hadn't decided to rob a bank just then, Avi and I would probably have criminal records!

So those Key West cops take the local laws seriously. That afternoon, Avi and I were trying to relax on a little beach downtown when the cops hauled away some poor soul for sleeping! Overall, I guess it's just a friendlier town for the kind of visitors who can afford to stay in a hotel. If you're wondering what Avi and I did the next night, well, we slept in a parking lot—in shifts. Then we took a bus back to Ohio.

Joel Whitaker '97
Oberlin College
Oberlin, OH

Who Partakes

Despite its small size and relative lack of beach, Key West attracts a substantial number of spring breakers. Floridians and Carolinians are particularly well-represented. Tough under-age drinking laws have thinned the ranks of the freshman and sophomore set, but many still come anyway.

In 1996, the Key West Business Guild inaugurated "Gay Spring Break," officially inviting gay and lesbian students to join the party. The event was not exactly a stretch for the town, which has a large year-round gay population and hosts thousands of gay and lesbian tourists every year. Still, the gesture was significant because of its singularity. No other spring break hot spot has rolled out a welcome mat, much less a "rainbow carpet" for gay and lesbian students.

"Gay Spring Break," which runs through Key West's entire five-week spring break season, features many of the same activities that are popular with straight students, including volleyball tournaments, pool parties and barbecues. A few activities, such as same-sex, clothing-optional cruises, are exclusive to gay students.

Alcohol Policy

To the chagrin of many spring breakers, Key West officials extend none of the city's trademark tolerance to under-age drinking. Those who try to get into bars with fake IDs are liable to end up picking up trash for a day as part of a community service sentence handed down by the town's unique Spring Break Court. (See *The Fake ID Blues* in Part 1.) While some students charge that Key West uses Spring Break Court to get free labor, the fact is, it seems to do the job. In 1994, 466 students reported to Spring Break Court. The number dropped to 267 by 1996.

Getting Around

Unlike most of its spring break counterparts, Key West is better suited to pedestrians than motorists. The streets are narrow, park-

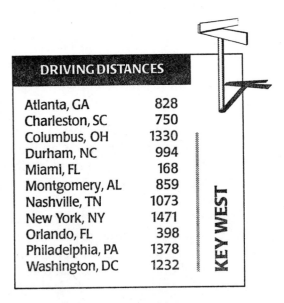

DRIVING DISTANCES	
Atlanta, GA	828
Charleston, SC	750
Columbus, OH	1330
Durham, NC	994
Miami, FL	168
Montgomery, AL	859
Nashville, TN	1073
New York, NY	1471
Orlando, FL	398
Philadelphia, PA	1378
Washington, DC	1232

KEY WEST

ing is scarce and gas is expensive. There are two bus routes around Key West. The first picks up in Old Town and goes clockwise around the island. The second picks up in Mallory Square and goes counterclockwise around the island. The fare is 75 cents for adults and 35 cents for students. For excursions outside of compact Old Town, bicycles and mopeds are common modes of transport.

KEY WEST WEB RESOURCES

Key West Online
http://www.vacation3.com/
A compilation of practical and fun Key West links, covering everything from weather and moped rental to the island's mock succession from the United States.

Key West Paradise
http://www.keywestparadise.com/
Another nice mix of useful and wacky, this site perfectly reflects the off-beat and eclectic nature of Key West.

Key West FAQ
http://members.aol.com/KeyWestFAQ/index.html
Authored by a witty local, here you can peruse an insider's Top-Ten-Things-To-Do list, find out which famous people live on the island or snag a recipe (you have your choice of six) for Key Lime Pie.

Gay Key West
http://www.gaykeywestfl.com/
A comprehensive guide for gay visitors to Key West, featuring a list of exclusively gay, and gay-friendly guest houses and inns.

SOUTH PADRE ISLAND

"Hey, Let's Padre!" Come spring break, such is the battle cry in this south Texas barrier isle. Its tropical environs, proximity to Mexico, and the permissiveness of local authorities have made it a March-time mecca for thousands of spring break pilgrims from the South and Midwest. Up until the mid-eighties, Padre Island was a well-kept secret among Texas students. Then, as local oil became less profitable and shrimp fewer, tourism became priority numero uno for the community. Soon, word about the island's spring break reputation spread and out-of-staters began to pour in. These days, Padre is one of the "Big Three" spring break destinations, joining Florida cronies, Panama City and Daytona Beach. Sure, plenty of cars still bear Texas A&M and UT bumper stickers, but just as many tout schools in Oklahoma, Kansas and Louisiana.

77°

Avg March
HIGH

At the Beach

Although Padre's beach is 34 miles long, breakers tend to congregate around the Hilton Hotel, the Sheraton Beach Resort and Charlie's Paradise Bar. (Remember, spring break is not complete without a dip in Charlie's guitar-shaped pool.) At the latter two, students will find Bacchus and Gamma's diversions, which include gladiator jousting, rock wall climbing and ersatz sumo wrestling. If these activities don't sate your inner adrenaline junkie, you'd better head to the bungee tower "in" Louie's Backyard. Or you can hope that ESPN is hosting another "Destination Extreme" event on Padre. This competition features aggressive inline skating, skateboarding and free-style bicycling. Whether you're an extreme sports enthusiast (You've heard of Tony Hawk.) or a complete novice (Inverted aerial, say what?), it's an event well worth checking out.

South of the Border Sojourns

When Mother Nature sticks you with a cloudy day on Padre, take a jaunt down to Matamoros, Mexico. It's just a hop (from Padre to Port Isabel), a skip (down to Brownsville) and a jump (over the Rio Grande) away, about 30 miles all told. Even better, no passport is needed. Matamoros' biggest attractions are its mercado (market) and its bars.

At the bustling mercado, which is about two miles from the border bridge, vendors hawk everything from colorful Mexican blankets to cowboy boots and silver jewelry. Because alcohol, like most things in Matamoros, is cheap by American standards, spring breakers also flock to the town's bars. While the brand of beer may change from Coors to Corona, it's basically the same frat party as on Padre. Most vendors, shops and bars in Matamoros accept U.S. dollars, but don't be surprised if they jack up the exchange rate a little. Remember, bartering is the norm at the mercado. If you accept the first asking price, you're probably paying too much.

Getting to Matamoros

Most spring breakers opt to drive to Brownsville and park (either in the University of Texas-Brownsville lot or the Jacob Brown Auditorium lot), then walk over the bridge to Mexico. Pedestrians pay 25 cents to cross the bridge to Matamoros, and 35 cents to return. Motorists pay $1 to go, and $1.50 to return. Once there, those on foot can use taxis, Maxi Taxis, or the free bus to get around. The trick with taxis, since most don't have meters, is to make sure you negotiate a fare before you get in. (By the way, tipping is standard.) Yellow Maxi Taxi buses are everywhere and usually go within a few blocks of the mercado. They cost 35 cents and can be flagged down with a wave. The free bus travels only to the mercado.

Nightlife on Padre

If you want live music on Padre, stake out Charlie's Paradise Bar. There, you'll find concerts almost every night during peak spring break season. In 1997, long-forgotten rapper Vanilla Ice surfaced at Charlie's, and even managed to rile the crowd a bit. Other artists, including Jackopierce, Quad City DJ's and Travis Tritt also appeared. The Bahia Mar resort also sponsors nightly concerts. If you're a theme fiend, you'll like Barracudas. It's got "foaming dance floor" night, "Trashed Disco" night and "Padre Pardi Gras," night. Louie's Backyard also digs a good New Orleans-style party and throws one every Tuesday through March. In addition, Louie's sponsors such titillating events as the "All Night Love" contest and the "Mind Eraser" contest.

When you start feeling a little "been there, done that" about nightlife on Padre, head down to Matamoros. It might not be a huge change of pace, but at least the beer's cheaper. Hop on one of the nightly "party buses" that run between Padre and Matamoros, and you won't have to worry about parking hassles or designated driver issues.

Who Partakes

The throngs on Padre largely reflect the demographics of the Midwest. In other words, there is no shortage of fair-haired, light-skinned spring breakers on the island, all bleaching their locks blonder and tanning their skins darker. While students of color make up a small number of Padre's breakers, as a whole, the spring break mass stands in sharp contrast to the heavily Latino, mostly working class communities of Padre and Port Isabel.

Alcohol Policy

Island District Court Judge David K. Colwell summed up the prevailing attitude toward spring break drinking when he warned, "No bottles on the beach, kegs and cans only. And if you're too drunk to walk, don't go stumbling through town." (Darn those hard-line Texans!) Indeed, Padre Island is one of the few places you can have a keg delivered to you on the beach.

Although Padre's rules are fairly lax, underage drinking is not ignored. During spring break, officers of the Texas Alcoholic Beverage Commission patrol the beach 12 hours a day handing out tickets to youth imbibers. Still, the measure isn't much of a deterrent, since students can always high-tail it to nearby Matamoros, where the drinking age is 18. Because drink is so cheap in Mexico, many spring breakers lug cases of Corona and bottles of tequila back over the border with them for consumption later. Under-aged drinkers, of course, get no such privileges.

Getting Around

Padre Island is connected to the mainland by the 2 mile Queen Isabella Causeway. Since during the height of the season, the bridge can get congested, it's best to stay on the island itself. Otherwise, you could be stuck doing the "Causeway Crawl" every time you want to go to the beach. Once on the island, the trolley that runs along Gulf Boulevard, Padre's main street, will get you around both day and night. If you're hanging at Charlie's, you can also take advantage of the "Must Bus," which provides free rides to patrons.

DRIVING DISTANCES	
Albuquerque, NM	1116
Austin, TX	361
Dallas, TX	555
Denver, CO	1244
Houston, TX	363
Kansas City, KS	1095
Lincoln, NE	1182
Little Rock, AR	884
New Orleans, LA	721
Oklahoma City, OK	750
St. Louis, MO	1252

PADRE ISLAND

PADRE ISLAND WEB RESOURCES

South Padre Island Convention and Visitors Bureau
http://www.sopadre.com
This friendly site contains the basics for all visitors, plus a special section about spring break.

The Alternative South Padre Island Page
http://www.south-padre-island.com
The unofficial dirt on spring break and South Padre, plus some "Good Advice from Mike McNamara: Island Lawyer."

Sons of the Beach
http://www.unlitter.com
Kept up by the Island's unique sand castle building club, this page features info about Padre and sand castles, plus the witty commentary of local yokel Sandy Feet.

LAKE HAVASU CITY

81°
Avg March HIGH

We have Mother Nature to thank for the picturesque beaches at most spring break destinations, but not Lake Havasu City. This western Arizona resort town was all Uncle Sam's doing. With the help of his Federal Bureau of Reclamation, he dammed up the Colorado River in 1938 and created the lake that gives the city its name. Havasu began its spring break run in the early eighties, but really got hot when MTV came to town in 1995. Students from all over the West flocked there for the event and although MTV did not return the next year, thousands of spring breakers did.

Boater's Paradise

When it comes to the spring break scene at Lake Havasu, lake is the operative word. This is not a place for the land-lubber, as much of the partying here happens on boats: houseboats, pontoon boats, sailboats, motor boats, rowboats, rafts and any other water crafts that students can borrow, rent or rig up. It's no surprise that drunk boating is actually more of a worry in Havasu than drunk driving. Oftentimes, marinas and coves are jammed with breakers aboard their docked vessels, drinking, sunning and boat-hopping. Copper Canyon, a cove off the lake, is a particularly popular place to drop anchor. It's also a favorite with daredevils who enjoy diving from the canyon's 60-foot cliffs.

On land, the London Bridge Resort and the Nautical Inn are the two major spring break hot spots in Havasu. (The former is so named because it looks onto Lake Havasu's very own span of the original London Bridge.) At either one you'll find a self-contained spring break world, where you can stumble out of bed and onto a wave runner as easily as you can stumble off the beach and into a night club.

If there's one thing you can count on in Lake Havasu, it's the weather. Rarely a day goes by that's not warm and sunny. (During spring break '97, the temperature actually hit a record-breaking 100°.) What about rain? Actually, it does happen in Havasu, maybe a half dozen times a year. Chances are, you'll miss any such meteorological phenomenon.

Nightlife in Havasu

For those who want to stay in town, Kokomos (part of the London Bridge Resort) and the Tiki Terrace (part of the Nautical Inn) are where it's at for spring breakers. Both showcase live bands throughout spring break. For breakers with money to burn, Nevada, in all its gaming glory, lies just a short drive away. Laughlin, located about an hour north of Havasu, is a miniature version of Las Vegas, and a favorite spot for breakers.

Who Partakes

Lake Havasu breakers reign from all over the West, but the largest contingents come from Arizona, California, Colorado, Nevada, New Mexico and Utah. Most are white students, ages 18 to 24.

Alcohol Policy

Alcohol is permitted on most of Lake Havasu's beaches. Drinking on boats is legal as well, though driving a boat while intoxicated is not.

Getting Around

Most spring breakers drive to Havasu, but once in town, a car is rarely necessary. Most attractions are within walking distance of the major spring break hotels and the city usually offers shuttle service for popular spring break events. What you should really have in Havasu is a boat, if not because it's absolutely necessary to get around, because it's an ideal way to enjoy the natural beauty of the

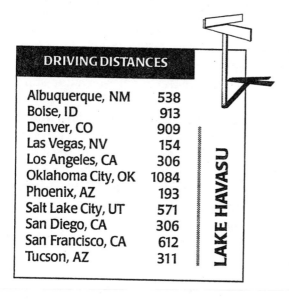

DRIVING DISTANCES	
Albuquerque, NM	538
Boise, ID	913
Denver, CO	909
Las Vegas, NV	154
Los Angeles, CA	306
Oklahoma City, OK	1084
Phoenix, AZ	193
Salt Lake City, UT	571
San Diego, CA	306
San Francisco, CA	612
Tucson, AZ	311

LAKE HAVASU

area. If you aren't able to transport the old trawler you keep in your dorm room, never fear, rental boats are abundant.

LAKE HAVASU WEB RESOURCES

Lake Havasu Virtual Community
http://www.lakehavasucity.com
While not as comprehensive as it could be, this site is the best one going in Lake Havasu. It contains map links, news and information on local recreation and nightlife.

Lake Havasu City Community Pages
http://www.havasu.com/
This could be an informative and interesting site if it ever gets off the ground.

Lake Havasu City Convention and Visitors Bureau
http://www.amdest.com/az/LHC/LHCCVB/vacation.html
This site contains the most basic of basics on Lake Havasu.

SPRING BREAK SIDE TRIPS

"Houston We Have a Problem."

For those of you who thought the movie "Apollo 18" was positively riveting, a trip to the Kennedy Space Center (KSC) at Cape Canaveral might be in order this spring break. Located on Florida's East Coast, it's any easy day trip from both Daytona Beach (91 miles) and Fort Lauderdale (171 miles). At Spaceport USA, KSC's main tourist attraction, visitors can learn about American space history, view the massive Saturn V rocket and watch IMAX movies on a five-story screen.

If you're lucky, your spring break trip will coincide with a shuttle launch. One recent spring breaker who spent his vacation in Daytona declared the 3 a.m. launch he saw at Cape Canaveral the best part of his trip. For a recorded message detailing upcoming launch dates, call NASA at (407) 867-4636 or check KSC's Office of Public Affairs web page at: http://www-pao.ksc.nasa.gov/kscpao/kscpao.htm. Currently, there is only one manned shuttle launch planned for next spring. As part of mission STS-90, the space shuttle Columbia is set to take off on April 2, 1998.

NASA sells 1500 "Launch Viewing Opportunity" (LVO) tickets for each shuttle launch. Ticket-holders get bus transportation to an open air viewing site on KSC property. Tickets cost $10 and usually go on sale about five days before a launch. They must be purchased in person at the KSC Visitor Center Ticket Pavilion, which is open 9 a.m. to 5 p.m. seven days a week.

A limited number of car passes are also available for each shuttle launch. These can be obtained by sending a postcard with your name and address and the launch mission number to:

NASA Visitor Services
Mail Code: PA-Pass
Kennedy Space Center, FL 32899

It's best to write for car passes several months in advance. They are distributed on a first-come first-served basis.

The best viewing locations outside the Space Center are on the Indian River on U.S. 1 in Titusville, on S.R. 528 along the Banana River and along the ocean in Cocoa Beach (Home to the Original Ron Jon Surf Shop).

Spring Training

After a stretch of carousing in Daytona Beach, Fort Lauderdale or Lake Havasu, you'll probably need a day off. Why not spend an afternoon at the ballpark watching major league baseball? If you're in Florida, you'll be within a short drive of a city where spring training is in full gear. If you're in Arizona, you may have to make a weekend of it. Either way, tickets are dirt cheap. The best seats usually go for between $8 and $10, while bleacher seats run between $4 and $6. Unless a wildly popular team like the New York Yankees is playing, you should be able to buy tickets the day of the game.

The most complete source of spring training information is the Spring Training Baseball Yearbook, a $5 newsstand magazine which contains a full game schedule, ticket information and team stats. You can also check Major League Baseball's official web page at http://www.majorleaguebaseball.com/springtraining/

The Grapefruit League

This League consists of the nineteen teams stationed in Florida for spring training. Below is a list of teams headquartered in cities nearby popular spring break destinations.

Atlanta Braves	West Palm Beach
Baltimore Orioles	Fort Lauderdale
Boston Red Sox	Fort Myers
Florida Marlins	Melbourne
Houston Astros	Kissimmee
LA Dodgers	Vero Beach
Montreal Expos	West Palm Beach
Minnesota Twins	Fort Myers
New York Mets	Port St. Lucie

The Cactus League

This league consists of the eight teams that call Arizona home during spring training. (The Chicago White Sox are scheduled to join them in '98.) Below they are listed with their host cities. Nestled together, Tempe, Mesa, Phoenix and Peoria are all around 200 miles from Lake Havasu.

Anaheim Angels	Tempe
Chicago Cubs	Mesa
Colorado Rockies	Tucson
Milwaukee Brewers	Chandler
Oakland Athletics	Phoenix
San Diego Padres	Peoria
San Francisco Giants	Scottsdale
Seattle Mariners	Peoria

Get Your Mickey Mouse Fix

How better to complete a week of regression and self-indulgence than with a trip to Disney World? It's cheap and easy with a Disney Break Ticket, which gives college students (with a valid college ID) access to one of Disney's three theme parks (Magic Kingdom, Epcot Center or MGM Studios), plus entry to Pleasure Island at night. While Pleasure Island's version of nightlife is predictably gimmicky and pre-fab, semi-known bands like Geggy Tah and Panama do play at the Island's various clubs. Tickets for Disney Break cost about $30 and are available from mid-February to mid-April. Disney World is about a half hour from Orlando's International Airport, a likely layover stop for Panama City-goers, and about an hour and a half from Daytona Beach.

International Destinations

FIVE

Cancún, Mexico

Cancún is easily the most popular international spring break destination. This is, in no small part, because of its stunning white-sand beaches, which extend for miles along the crystal blue waters of the Caribbean. In terms of raw materials, Cancún's got it all. Unfortunately, the Mexican government has developed the resort ad nauseam, slapping glossy hotels on the beach like cheap spangles on an elegant dress. Still, American students (and other international tourists) like Cancún's reliability. They can always count on a sun-kissed week of tasty tropical drinks, pool side banter, and dancing till dawn. There are no shocks, but then there's not much serendipity either.

Most students come to Cancún through a tour company and stay at one of the many beach side hotels in the Zona Hotelera (hotel zone). While many opt to stay close by their hotel, the beaches are public and can be fun to roam. Most hotels pack the day with pool side games and activities, and usually offer snorkeling, jet-skiing and parasailing as well.

Nightlife in Cancún

Being the vacation station it is, Cancún has tons of clubs and bars, many of them tailored to (and priced for) its wealthy visitors. Most resound with a throbbing house beat, but you'll also find some reggae and American pop mixed in too. Particularly popular are Daddy-O's, Señor Frog's, Carlos 'n Charlie's, La Boom, Fat Tuesdays and Tequila Rock. Remember clubs here are open all night long, so be sure to catch a cat nap before you hit the town. Also, it's not a bad idea to eat dinner early at the bar-restaurant where you plan to start your drinking. After dinner, hang around while things change over and you'll avoid the long lines that form later in the evening.

Pyramids, Serpents and Human Sacrifice

Although it's not always evident from the manicured beaches and climate-controlled malls in Cancún, Mexico has a rich and colorful past. The best way to see this side of things is to break away for a day trip to a nearby archeological site like Chichén Itzá or Tulum. You might also check out the underwater caverns of Xel Ha Lagoon. Tour operators and hotels regularly organize trips to these destinations, all you have to do is board the bus.

Chichén Itzá, about 97 miles southwest of Cancún, houses the ruins of a Mayan city first settled between 500 and 900 AD, abandoned, then resettled around 1100 AD. After you walk around a bit and listen to the tour guide's sensationalized stories, scale the steep El Castillo pyramid for an adrenaline rush and an excellent aerial view of the area. (Be sure to have your picture taken during your climb, the pyramid's side will look almost vertical and you'll look like spiderman.) For those visiting at the spring equinox (March 21), look at the north staircase side of El Castillo. The Mayan architects designed the pyramid so that a series of triangular shadows would suggest a serpent slithering down at this time. (The same phenomenon also occurs at the fall equinox.) Also interesting, is the principal ball court, just northwest of El Castillo. Look carefully at the wall reliefs, you'll bear witness to the gruesome decapitation of the losing players.

About 79 miles south of Cancún is Tulum, built on a cliff overlooking the beach. There, you'll find the ruins of a smaller ancient Mayan City built between 1200 and 1400 AD. Again, the focal point is El Castillo, a temple built atop a tall pyramid. Make the ascent and you'll get a great view of the Caribbean, as well as of the jungle and ruins. The Temple of the Frescoes and the Temple of the Diving Gods are also worth a look. Just north of Tulum is the Xel Ha Lagoon National Park. There, you can rent snorkel equipment and check out the tropical angelfish, parrotfish and coral that inhabit the underground caverns. Because Xel Ha does get crowded with snorkelers, don't be surprised if you have to deflect an occasional elbow or knee.

Getting Around

After the Zona Hotelera, you'll probably spend most of your time in the centro (downtown) shopping, eating or clubbing. Buses designated "hoteles" or "centro" travel between the two from 5 a.m. to 1 a.m. In lieu of the bus, take one of Cancún's abundant taxis. Just make sure you settle on the fare before you accept the ride. Bargaining is acceptable.

Money

Generally, it's best to change your dollars into pesos once you arrive in Mexico. You can do so either at banks, casas de cambio (money-changing offices) or often, major hotels. You'll probably get the best exchange rate at banks, though they may charge a 2% to 5% commission for traveler's checks. Casas de cambio, which stay open into the evening, are a convenient, though more expensive alternative. Typically, hotels gouge money-changing tourists, either by offering terrible exchange rates or charging ridiculous commissions.

ATM machines, when they work, are a good source of fast cash. The exchange rates on such transactions are usually fair, though you never know when the ubiquitous commission will show its face. In Mexico, ATM cards on the Cirrus and PLUS network are most often accepted.

Cancún Web Resources

Cancún
http://www.yucatanweb.com/
This site is the starting point for guides to Cancún and several other Yucatan cities. The Cancún page features 22 categories, covering everything from spring break specials to Mayan ruins.

Cancún: The User's Guide
http://www.caribe.net.mx/siegel/nofrdir.htm
Billed as Cancún's "only 100% independent local guide," this site boasts an eclectic mix of topics, from "Nightlife" to "Ice Cream." It seems to be written from an American ex-patriot's perspective.

Jamaica

In 1989, the Jamaican Tourist Bureau (JTB) began sponsoring spring break events to attract American students. It worked. Today, thousands of breakers travel to Jamaica during March and April, all eager to trade in their Coors for Red Stripe and their Kentucky Fried for jerk chicken. For most, Jamaica lives up to its reputation as the sultry, laid back land of rastas and reggae. Its beaches are not as big or beautiful as Mexico's, but it's got a personality that's hard to resist. Treat yourself to a week in Montego Bay or Negril and you'll be chilling halfway into next quarter, rising to any occasion with a hearty, "No problem, mon!"

Getting the Hustle

Jamaica is known for its legion of street hustlers, who accost tourists at every opportunity, hawking jewelry, wood-carvings, t-shirts, trinkets, ganja, aloe vera rubs, and sex (to both men and women). They will also offer to serve as a guide or change your money. They are brazen and persistent. Women offering aloe vera rubs on the beach will often forgo a sales pitch and start massaging sunbathers' legs unsolicited. Many private resorts bar hustlers from their beaches, but this hasn't stopped hustlers from paddling up in kayaks or on surfboards. The best way to handle the unwanted hustler is to respond with a definitive "No thanks!" This will usually do the trick, though some might suggest that you've offended or disrespected them. Stand your ground, be polite and, if possible, diffuse the situation with humor.

Ganja

Ganja, (marijuana) is illegal in Jamaica, but you wouldn't know it. Street hustlers offer spliffs or bags at every turn and most road side venders keep some on hand. Many households have ganja plots and inland farmers tend gigantic ganja plantations, the product of which mostly ends up in the United States. Despite its status as an illegal drug, ganja doesn't have the same contraband stigma it carries in the States. Practicing Rastafarians see ganja as a tool for their faith, and use it to seek God and find inner clarity. But it's more than a religious accessory. Much of the general population, from the wealthy upper class to the impoverished majority, use ganja regularly.

Whether to partake or not is your choice, but there's no denying that you will have ample opportunity to inhale. In fact, it may be downright impossible to avoid a contact high if you're in the thick of things at one of the outdoor music festivals so popular in Jamaica. If you decide to abstain, a firm "No, thanks!" ought to keep the hustlers at bay. If you decide to take your chances, beware! You will not be spared fines or even imprisonment because you're a foreigner. The police regularly arrest tourists for possessing ganja and have no qualms about punishing them as they would Jamaicans.

Money

Jay, the Jamaican dollar is the official currency, but American dollars are widely accepted. Still, it's wise to have some jay with you just in case. You can exchange money in banks, which have the best rates, or in licensed exchange bureaus. Hustlers will also offer to change your money, but it's a risky venture, as they are not known for their honesty.

Jamaica Web Resources

Jamaican Tourist Board (JTB)
http://www.jamaicatravel.com
This crisp, colorful site covers all bases. You'll get the quick dirt on resorts (including Montego Bay and Negril), weather, festivals and water sports.

De Site on Jamaica
http://www.jamaicans.com/jam.htm
This "unofficial" Jamaica site gently razzes tourists while informing them about the island's culture, people, food and language. Don't miss the "Real Jamaican Tourist" section or the list of Jamaica links.

Montego Bay

Located on the northeast coast, Montego Bay is Jamaica's second largest city (after Kingston) and biggest resort area. It's more cosmopolitan than Negril, but doesn't have the same flair for extreme leisure. Still, it's a better place for the breaker who wants variety. Between the shops and bars of Gloucester Avenue, the stately historic buildings clustered around Church Street and the beach, there is scads to do in MoBay. In addition, MoBay is a good departure point for day trips to other parts of the island, including Negril.

Beach Tips

All-inclusive resorts have the best beaches in MoBay. If a pleasant, roomy, mostly hustler-free beach is a priority, these are the accommodations for you. Otherwise, Dr. Cave's Beach, and to a lesser extent, Cornwall Beach are the ones to hit. The wider Dr. Cave's is the main MoBay beach and caters to both locals and tourists. Unfortunately, it is separated from the city by an ugly concrete wall. North of Dr. Cave's is the much smaller Cornwall Beach, whose focal point is the Bird Watcher's Bar. It also suffers from an unsightly barrier, a tall chain-link fence around its perimeter. Beach-goers must pay a small entrance fee at both.

Get Out of Town!

Negril usually tops the MoBay breaker's list of "extra-curriculars." Only 52 miles southwest of Montego Bay, it's an easy day trip and the sunsets alone make it worthwhile. In the other direction, Ocho Rios, and its main attraction, Dunn's River Falls are popular. Ochi, as the locals call it, is 67 miles east of MoBay and a typical resort town, with the usual line-up of hotels on the beach, cruise ships in the port and duty-free stores in town. At nearby Dunn's River Falls, adventurous visitors can scramble up the cascade's massive rock tiers rising 600 feet above the beach. Daintier types walk up the wooden stairs along side the falls.

Not many spring break packages include excursions to the Appleton Distillery, but you should make the trip south to Maggoty, if possible. For about $12, you can take a factory tour, which includes a video and a blow-by-blow account of rum-making through the ages. (Home brewers, you'll appreciate this!) Afterwards, you'll sample various rums and get a bottle to take back with you.

Nightlife in MoBay

If you're staying at an all-inclusive resort, you may be perfectly happy to keep to the rum-swilling, limbo-watching carnival inside. If you get restless though, there's plenty to do downtown. Walter's, the Dead End Beach Bar and Margaritaville are popular drinking holes frequented by both tourists and locals. If you're more in the mood for blasting reggae on the beach, there's probably a boonoonoonoos, or beach party, going on somewhere. Try Cornwall Beach, Walter Fletcher Beach, Gloucester Avenue or Dead End Beach. If you want to "ride de riddims" all night long, dance on over to the Cave or Pier One.

Getting Around

MoBay is a pedestrian-friendly city as long as you stick to the beaten path between Gloucester Avenue and downtown. Otherwise, take a taxi or rent a motorbike. There is no public transportation.

Negril

Negril is as mellow as it gets in Jamaica. Tourists and locals smoke ganja openly, hallucinogenic mushrooms are omelette ingredients (they are legal), and tan lines are a choice not a matter of course. In the sixties and seventies, this small, then-undiscovered village was a favorite among hippies. (Go figure!) Today, it is a booming resort, popular with North American and European vacationers who want to live it up and let it all hang out. They've certainly picked the right place.

Life's the Beach

In Negril, just about everything starts on or from the beach, at least during the day. If you're not baking on the sand or checking out the craft stalls, you'd best be making good use of Negril's calm, clear waters. Sailboards, Sunfish and jet skis are popular and are available from beach concessionaires, if not from your hotel. Negril's coral reefs and their abundance of sea life make it a great place for snorkeling. Even better though, is scuba diving, which beginners can try for about $50 at many resorts. The underground grottos, coral reefs and off-shore plane wrecks make for fascinating underwater adventures. (Do not hire a "free-lancer" off the beach to take you diving. Instead, opt for a resort-sponsored course or a session offered by scuba professionals.)

When you're sick of being stared at by octopi, barracuda and nurse sharks, get out of the water and onto a boat. In a sea kayak you can glide noiselessly through the shallows of the area's hidden beaches and coves. For something closer to an amusement park ride, climb aboard a banana boat, which is an inflatable raft pulled behind a speed boat. Finally, there is the party boat, an unsinkable island break institution. Such excursions usually take about 2 to 3 hours and include all the drink you can down.

Nightlife in Negril

First, drop by Rick's to watch Negril's phenomenal raspberry mango sunsets. The bar is a local institution and is always jammed for the nightly ritual. If you're a reggae fan, Negril is the best place you can be during spring break. In mid-March, Hog Heaven Hotel hosts the celebrated West End Reggae Festival, featuring such artists as Ziggy Marley, Third World and Yellow Man. De Buss, Kaiser's and MXIII also host weekly live shows showcasing similar caliber talents. If you want to break in your dancing shoes, Compulsion, or Private Affair in Hotel Samsara will probably do the job. If you're in a bar mood, try the Pickled Parrot or Alfred's Ocean Palace.

Getting Around

It is not practical to depend on your feet to get you around Negril, which has a developed coast line about ten miles long. Several resorts provide free shuttle service into town. If yours doesn't, spring for a taxi or rent a scooter, motorbike or bicycle.

Nassau, The Bahamas

Here, you get a Caribbean vacation with the ease of being in the States. That's not to say that Nassau might as well be Miami, just that there are no language barriers, currency conundrums or major cultural differences to deal with. Spring break in the Bahamian capital means a week flush with beach time, party cruises, shopping sprees and gambling. It's a trip perfectly suited to fun-loving students who can overlook the city's cruise ship glut and development deluge.

The Lay of the Land

Nassau's Tourist Triangle:

- Downtown Nassau, home to the cobbled historic district, the shopping district, the straw market and many bars and restaurants.
- Cable Beach, a resort-lined four-mile stretch just west of Nassau. Its beach is far superior to Nassau's measly Western Esplanade Beach.
- Paradise Island, a stone's throw north of Nassau. It is known for its beaches, its natural beauty, its casino and its snobby attitude.

Eat, Drink, Eat, Buy Straw and Get Braids

All-inclusive resorts aren't the rage in Nassau like they are in Negril and MoBay. Thus, most packages won't come with extras like drinks, water-sports and private parties. Then again, there's a lot more to do in Nassau than play volleyball and go snorkeling.

If you decide to play the explorer for a day or two, don't miss Arawak Cay, a small man-made island just over Bay Street, which is Nassau's main beach side drag. There, you can nibble fresh conch (an ocean mollusk in the snail family), just snatched from the sea, and wash it down with a local drink made with gin and coconut milk. If you crave a more conventional beverage, head to the Bacardi Distillery for a tour and a chance to sample some good old-fashioned rum. The distillery is located on Millars Sound in south New Providence, about ten miles away from downtown Nassau.

Back in town, Potter's Cay, under the bridge leading to Paradise Island, is another colorful stop. There, you'll see locals out to market amidst stands brimming with fresh fruits and vegetables, and docked boats with just-caught fish and conch. When you've had enough food and drink, move onto the Straw Market for souvenirs and products made from (Yep, you guessed it!) straw. It's a good time to practice your bargaining skills. After you've "done straw," consider getting a new do at the open-air Hairbraider's Centre on Prince George Dock. Surprisingly, this mini-convention of braiding pros is a government-sponsored initiative.

Nightlife in Nassau

Don't feel bad if you have a Love Boat flashback when night falls in Nassau. It happens. Shake the feeling with a nice slot-playing jag at one of the two area casinos. Atlantis Paradise Island Casino is the bigger and snazzier of the two, though Crystal Palace Casino on Cable Beach gives it a good run for *your* money. (The gambling age is 21 in the Bahamas.)

In Nassau itself, the BahaMen Culture Club is a good choice if you want to dance to junkanoo, a signature Bahamian music combining skin or steel drums, cowbells, whistles, piano, guitar and electric base. Club Waterloo and the Goombay Club are also hopping joints. Between Nassau and Cable Beach is the Zoo, a five-bar club with themes ranging from Gilligan's Island to ESPN worship. Finally, ensconced between two resort hotels on Cable beach, is the Rock and Roll Cafe, a Hard Rock imitation with loud music and a youngish crowd.

Getting Around

It's easy to see Nassau on foot, and it's even possible to walk to neighboring attractions like Cable Beach and Paradise Island. (Walking in downtown Nassau at night is not a good idea.) Buses, called jitneys, are also an option, especially when you're trying to reach other parts of the island. The fare is 75 cents and exact change is required. For day trips to Paradise Island, water-taxis are a good buy at $3 per round trip. Regular taxis, which are usually unmarked minivans, are also inexpensive.

For some reason, Bahamians don't put much stock in street numbers or street names. Thus, don't rely on addresses to get you where you're going. Ask directions, most locals will gladly help.

Money

For once, money is a cinch. The Bahamian dollar is equivalent to the American dollar and both are accepted throughout the country. Both Cirrus and PLUS network ATM machines are found in The Bahamas, especially in big cities like Nassau.

Bahamas Web Resources

The Bahamas Official Travel Guide
http://www.interknowledge.com/bahamas/bshome01.htm
Sponsored by The Bahamas Ministry of Tourism, this site covers Bahamian destinations as well as standard tourist information.

The Bahamas
http://thebahamas.com/
This site profiles the major cities and islands of the Bahamas, and contains hotel and restaurant information. Out of the blue is "MANIFESTO II," the "agenda for the 21st century" of the currently ruling Free National Movement.

Part Two   **Slopeside Breaks**

Snow Schemes

SIX

So you make a beeline for the little neighborhood ski hill every chance you get? Driving 50 or 100 miles so you can come back to campus with a slopeful of perfectly-carved turns to your name? Hoping one of these days to touch down on a real mountain where big-time schussmeisters play? Wondering what it feels like to ease into a hot tub at the end of the day or trade war stories over après-ski fare? It sounds like your number's up for a ski vacation. Forget the beach this year and high-tail it to the slopes.

You don't have to be a pro to have a great time skiing over spring break. Beginners often love such trips because they improve dramatically over a very short period. Plus, there's lots more to a ski trip than skiing. That's what après-ski is all about, whether it involves jacuzzi jams, bar-crawls or barbecues. Remember, even trips to such legendary wintertime playgrounds as Vail or Lake Tahoe don't have to set you back a semester's worth of tuition. Many tour operators offer good deals to students, especially to those who plan early. Our only caveat: After a week on the slopes, you may be ready to drop out of school, pick up a resort job and ski yourself into the fifth dimension. Better start priming the 'rents.

The Shredding Alternative

Snowboarders accomplished what some of the steepest, twistiest, iciest slopes couldn't. They scared skiers, flying out of the ether like hit-and-run drivers. Just when a messy crash seemed imminent, they'd swerve deftly out of the way. Skiers scorned these snow-surfing demons and nodded smugly as resorts shooed the hellions off the slopes or relegated them to tiny, out-of-the-way snowboard parks.

But snowboarding was no flash in the pan. Today, even as the number of skiers continues to decline, the shredder's ranks are swelling. And it's not just Gen-Xers who are flocking to the sport. Plenty of veteran skiers are giving it a shot and there's bound to be an all-around shredding explosion once snowboarding makes its Olympic debut in Japan in 1998. Gradually, resorts have come to accept their new patrons. Most now welcome boarders and many have added state-of-the-art snowboard parks or half-pipes for them. Aspen Mountain (but not Snowmass, Buttermilk or Aspen Highlands,) Taos and Alta are among the only major resorts closed to shredders.

The Boarder's Learning Curve

Learning to snowboard is literally a pain in the butt. And if you don't get some nasty bruises in that region, you're a hardy specimen indeed. Snowboarding can also be rough on the wrists and knees, due to the full-acceleration face plants that beginners tend to execute so well. Rest assured, the snowboarder's learning curve is steep, steeper than a skier's usually. In other words, it won't be very long (maybe a day and a half) until you glide smoothly off the lift instead of wiping out the second your board touches the ground. Once you get the hang of snowboarding, there's no going back. It's beautifully simple and fluid, yet fast and thrilling, too.

Ski Tour Operators

Tour operators can make your trip to the slopes easier and cheaper than if you organized it yourself. Below are just a few of the tour operators that organize spring break ski trips. Keep in mind that all price estimates are just that, estimates. Always call for the most up-to-date rates.

Moguls Ski and Snowboard Tours
Boulder, CO
1-800-666-4857
http://www.skimoguls.com/
Destinations: .... All major western resorts, some eastern
Low-end price estimate for
   4-day lift ticket and
   5-night stay: $259-380
Free Trips: .... 1 for every 15-20 sign-ups.

Sports America Tours

Santa Rosa, CA
1-800-876-8551
http://sportsamerica.com
Destinations: .... All major western resorts, a few in
Minnesota

Low-end price estimate for
4-day lift ticket and
5-night stay: $281-356
Free Trips: .... 1 for every 15-20 sign-ups.

Sunchase Tours

Fort Collins, CO
1-800-SUNCHASE
http://www.sunchase.com
Destinations: .... Steamboat, Breckenridge,
Keystone-Arapahoe Basin, Vail

Low-end price estimate for
4-day lift ticket and
5-night stay: $266
Free Trips: .... 1 for every 15 sign-ups.

Breakaway Tours

Toronto, Canada
1-800-465-4257
http://www.breakawaytours.com
Destinations: .... Vermont, Québec
Low-end price estimate for
4-day lift ticket and
5 night stay: $215
Free Trips: .... 1 for every 15-20 sign-ups.

Student Adventure Travel

Dallas City, IL
1-800-711-2604
http://www.studentadvtrav.com
Destinations: .... Colorado and other major western
resorts

Low-end price estimate for
  4-day lift ticket and
  5 night stay: .... $259-$279
Free Trips: .... 1 for every 12-25 sign-ups.

Don't wait until after Christmas vacation to start planning your
spring break ski trip. If you do, you could get stuck in some crummy
condo half an hour away from the slopes. The sooner you book your
trip, the better chance you'll have of securing affordable ski-in ski-
out accommodations. For the best deals, start calling tour operators
or the resorts themselves in October or November.

Skiing the Web

SkiNet
http://www.skinet.com/
Sponsored by the publishers of Ski Magazine and Skiing Magazine,
this site is appealing and informative. It includes numerous articles
from both magazines, a list of top resorts and good bargains, plus,
a special section for women skiers.

Ski Central
http://skicentral.com
This index of all things skiing and snowboarding is comprehensive
with a capital C. It contains over 4000 links, but is well-organized
enough not to overwhelm.

GoSki
http://www.goski.com
This is the place to peruse resort guides, gear reviews, skiing news
and travel information. It's also a good place to look up ski clubs
or check out slope-side weather.

Shredding the Web

Snowboardz.com
http://www.snowboardz.com/
No matter what you want to know about snowboards, snowboarding or snowboarders, Snowboardz.com will lead you to it. The
site is a crisp, complete and simple compendium of snowboard
web resources.

Frost
http://www.charged.com/frost
In the name of action sports and extreme leisure, Charged Magazine created this snowboarding e-zine. It's a neat publication with fantastic graphics (though a little heavy on the frames) and interesting features like "Board Cheap, Look Good."

Beauty
http://www.beauty.se/
Another boarding e-zine, this one from Sweden, Beauty has some absolutely stunning photos (it helps to have a fast modem), as well as a few video clips. Probably of less interest to Americans are snippets about Swedish boarding destinations and competitions.

Ski Resorts 101: A Survey  SEVEN

This 2-credit course highlights ski resorts on both sides of the country (and in Canada) that are popular with students during spring break. Students will learn about each resort's slopes, ambiance and après-ski offerings. Following the course, there will be an optional practicum to take place at the resort of the student's choice.

Vermont

Killington
1-800-372-2007
http://www.killington.com
Also known as King-K, Killington is the premier ski area in the East and a perfect spring break destination. Not only does it generally attract a young, power-bar crowd, it sponsors an Annual Collegiate Snowfest every March, just for breakers. Boasting six peaks and three separate base clusters, Killington is something of a giant. If you'd rather not be lost from the get-go, take a "Meet the Mountain" tour to familiarize yourself with the area. Skiers and boarders up through advanced will find plenty to keep them busy. Beginners and never-evers typically love the Killington experience because there are so many green runs starting from the summits. For once, they get the same thrilling views as the seasoned pros. Snowboarders are welcome on all trails at Killington and have their own half-pipe and board park. Shredders, keep your eyes open for the annual snowboard mogul contest held each spring.

Killington is not a village, but rather a sprawling collection of shops, condos, bars and eateries along Killington Road. While it's not set up for a pub crawl, a pub drive would certainly be appropriate. For instant après-ski libation, there is the Base Lodge and Pogonips at the mountain. Later, when you get your second wind, hotfoot it to the Wobbly Barn, the Pickle Barrel or Casey's Caboose.

Stowe

1-800-247-8693
http://www.stowe.com

Stowe Mountain Resort is vintage New England, from its narrow, serpentine trails to its historic brick and white clapboard buildings. Although Mount Mansfield is a shrimp compared to its towering Rocky Mountain cousins, it offers lots of quality skiing, plus a certain idyll missing out West. Stowe is well-suited to skiers and boarders of all ability levels. Although Stowe's snow-making system is fairly advanced, watch out for occasional patches of "New England ice." Snowboarders are permitted on all trails at Stowe and in the Flight Deck board park. There is night skiing on some runs (intermediate and above) until 10 p.m. Wednesday through Sunday.

Stowe will not overwhelm you with its après-ski scene, but it does have a few dependable bars and a number of good eatin' joints. The Matterhorn Bar on Mountain Road is always hopping, as is Mr. Pickwick's Polo Pub at the Olde England Inne and The Rusty Nail, which has live music most nights. Because Mt. Mansfield and the town of Stowe are 7 miles apart, a car is helpful. A trolley runs between the two ($1 one-way) until 11 p.m., but it's not known for its expedience.

Also: Conveniently located just down the road from Stowe is one of Vermont's true treasures, the Ben and Jerry's factory. Tours run every thirty minutes. The cost is $1.50.

Québec

Tremblant

819-681-2000
http://www.goski.com/rcan/trembla.htm

If someone slapped a new and improved sticker on this mountain, it would be altogether justified. In recent years, Tremblant has developed several new advanced and expert runs and installed a fancy new snow-making system as well as a plethora of new lifts. While the trails here tend to be narrow, there is terrain for all ability levels. Snowboarders are permitted everywhere and are bound to enjoy Tremblant's excellent snowboard park.

Tremblant is not near a major city, but between its base village and St.-Jovite, 6 miles away, skiers should have no problem finding après-ski diversions. Of course, it doesn't hurt that the drinking age is 18 in Québec.

Mont-Sainte-Anne

418-827-4561
http://www.goski.com/rcan/mtsa.htm
Overlooking the St. Lawrence River, this mountain is a beautiful place to ski and offers plenty of terrain for all ability levels, except maybe experts. It's also got one of the best lift systems in North America so there's rarely a wait, even on weekends when all of Québec City goes skiing. Snowboarders are welcome on almost all trails and can take advantage of a good-sized half-pipe and a board park.

The best thing about Mont-Sainte-Anne, beside its skiing, is its proximity to Québec City. With this French-flavored metropolitan hub only 25 miles away, there are any number of drinking, dancing and dining venues available for après-ski fun. Again, the drinking age in Québec is 18.

Colorado

Steamboat

1-800-922-2722
http://www.steamboat-ski.com
Although Steamboat is a shiny, modern resort, it still holds tight to its down-home cowboy past. This doesn't mean you'll dodge thundering horses on your way to the mountain, but you might find your lift attendant peering out from beneath a ten gallon hat. As for the slopes, they are varied and challenging for intermediate and advanced skiers, but not the best for beginners or never-evers. Most green runs are cat trails (narrow trails in the woods) that cut across advanced runs frequented by jet-fueled pros. The bunny hill, at the bottom of the mountain, suffers from the same problem, especially at the end of the day when everyone's heading home. Snowboarders are allowed on all trails here and have four board parks to choose from.

Between Steamboat Village (at the base) and Steamboat Springs, a few miles away, you'll find plenty to satisfy your après-ski needs. To soak away your aches and pains visit Strawberry Park Hot Springs, 10 miles north of the resort. Then head to Inferno, Dos Amigos, Heavenly Daze or Tugboat. All are happening nightspots, complete with peppy crowds and live music. A free shuttle bus runs between Steamboat Springs and the ski area every 20 minutes.

Crested Butte

1-800-544-8448
http://www.toski.com/crested/
With slopes this superb and a town this charming, Crested Butte could easily have itself a nice, juicy superiority complex. But while this may be the modus operandi at similarly endowed resorts, that's not the way things work here. Crested Butte prefers to deliver the goods with a nod and smile. And the crowd it attracts is much the same, low-key and casual, except, of course, when it comes to attacking the slopes. Extreme skiers are truly in their element here, but there is plenty for every ability level, on down to the greenest never-ever. Snowboarders are permitted everywhere at Crested Butte and can also tool around in the board park.

The après-ski action starts (and perhaps ends) at Rafters in Mount Crested Butte at the base of the mountain and later moves three miles down the road into Crested Butte itself. There, you'll find good bar-hopping terrain. Be sure to stagger into the Wooden Nickel, The Bistro, Kochevar's or the Idle Spur while you're out. No need to bring your car to Crested Butte, a free shuttle goes between the resort and town regularly, and cabs are cheap.

The Summit County Four

This county houses one of the ski world's best known foursomes: Breckenridge, Copper Mountain, Keystone and Arapahoe Basin, ensuring that visitors will absolutely, positively, never, ever run out of slopes to ski or things to do. Each resort has its own base village, except A-Basin, which doubles up with Keystone. Vail recently bought Breckenridge, Keystone and A-Basin and may create a universal lift ticket for the three. Consequently, Copper will probably keep its lift rates lower than its neighbors.

A free bus system called the Summit Stage runs between all three towns and all four ski areas throughout the day. If you don't stay at one of the three resorts, you might try Frisco, a small, funky town right in the middle of things. It is closest to Breckenridge and Copper Mountain, but the Keystone complex is hardly far away.

Breckenridge

1-800-784-7669
http://www.ski-breckenridge.com/breck.html
Being at the top of the ski-resort heap, Breckenridge does have something of a high brow element. Still, it's no Aspen and doesn't want to be. Mostly, it's just darn good at what it does, which is ski and après-ski. Spread over 4 peaks, Breckenridge offers its patrons a whole lot of mountain on which to cruise, carve, bump and jump. Best of all, there is plenty of terrain for all ability levels, from wide, well-groomed beginner slopes to some of the highest inbound runs in North America. Snowboarders are permitted on all trails and bowls, and, of course, in Breck's first-class snowboard park.

In addition to quality skiing, Breckenridge boasts a lively Victorian-hued town. Après-ski hot spots include Tiffany's and Copper Top in the Beaver Run Resort and Downstairs at Eric's and JohSha's in town. Although almost everything in Breckenridge is within walking distance, the free town trolley and bus system pick up regularly.

Copper Mountain

1-800-458-8386
http://www.ski-copper.com
Talk about an exquisitely organized ski mountain. Beginner, intermediate and advanced runs are neatly partitioned off so skiers and boarders at each ability level have the freedom to go as fast or slow as they want. Wisely placed chair lifts ensure that skiers are whisked efficiently up to the slopes. Overall, Copper provides fantastic skiing and you don't need an atlas to find it. Snowboarders are permitted on all sections of the mountain. They can also enroll in one or two-day snowboard camps, featuring both carving and freestyle instruction.

Copper Mountain's nightlife is not quite as exemplary as its skiing. The family-friendly setting keeps things rather subdued, but then Breck is just down the road. For immediate après-ski activity head to Kokomo's Bar in the Copper Commons or the B-lift Pub. For a good feed go to O'Shea's or Farley's.

Keystone

1-800-222-0188
http://www.ski-breckenridge.com/keyst.html
Keystone started out as a heavily forested area without much natural skiing terrain. Its relative lack of snow didn't help either. But with a lot of molding, shaping and grooming, not to mention a superstar snow-making system, Keystone has become a first rate ski resort, one that many locals swear by. There are runs here for all ability levels, but beginner and intermediate offerings are particularly ample. For those who can't get enough during the day, Keystone also offers night skiing until 9 p.m. A stubborn hold-out on the snowboard issue, Keystone finally began allowing shredders on its slopes last year. Its newest addition is a giant terrain board park.

Keystone, like Copper, is not known for its night life. For immediate après-ski, Last Lift Bar in the Mountain House is a popular stop. At night, Bandito's and the Snake River Saloon are good for a beer, but eventually it's off to Breck or Vail.

Arapahoe Basin

(See Keystone for Contact Information)
It has green and blue runs, but beginning and intermediate skiers are not who this 13,050 foot mountain was made for. Arapahoe was made for the skilled, gutsy, never-say-die kind of skier who can handle steeps, gullies and chutes, not to mention bitter cold temperatures and the occasional white-out.

While Keystone and Arapahoe are almost always mentioned in the same breath, they do not share a mountain. (They do share a lodging and base village at Keystone though.) Arapahoe is five miles from Keystone, a trip skiers and boarders make via a free shuttle.

Vail

1-800-525-2257
http://vail.net

Vail might as well be a superlative. It's always at the top of any resort rankings. It receives more visitors than any other American resort. It's got the biggest single ski mountain in North America, the biggest ski school in the world and the biggest high speed quad network of any resort in the country. It's also got a stylish, convenient resort village stocked with shops, restaurants and bars. With so much to be proud of, it's no surprise that Vail is pricey and stuck up. Nevertheless, if you have the bucks and a little bit of attitude, you'll fit right in.

Vail is huge and has enough to keep intermediate and advanced skiers or boarders busy for weeks. It's not so ideal for never-evers or beginners, however. Besides the fact that green runs are spread out, the profusion of upper-level skiers can be daunting. Boarders are 100% welcome at Vail and have two half-pipes, a board park and a ski/board terrain park to tackle.

Après-ski in Vail is a variety show. If you don't want to belly up to the bar right away, see a movie, check out the ski museum, go shopping or head to the ice rink. If you do want to belly up to the bar right away, you'll have your work cut out for you. In the Village, Sarah's and Vendetta's will get you started. For good live music later on, try The Club, Garton's Saloon, and on weekends Sundance Saloon and Jackalope. For the most part, walking will get you around Vail, but there is a free bus service just in case.

Purgatory

1-800-525-0892
http://www.ski-purg.com

You won't find many condescending ski-meisters or fashion sophisticates here, as Purgatory works hard to be the consummate commoner's resort. Overall, it's a friendly, laid-back place with great skiing and some of the cheapest rates around. Most skiers and boarders love the dip-peppered terrain, which makes a trip down the mountain rather like a roller coaster ride. Purgatory has plenty of runs for all ability levels except expert. Snow-boarders are permitted on almost everything except the family ski zone and one blue trail. They also have their own board park.

Farquahrts and Purgatory Creek are the best choices for après-ski activity at the resort. If you're craving a hot soak, try Trimble Hot Springs, 20 miles south. Later in the evening, head for Durango, 25 miles south. During spring break, things really heat up there, particularly at Farquahrts Bar (Farquahrts in-town counterpart) and the Sundance Saloon.

Wyoming

Jackson Hole
1-800-443-6931
http://www.jacksonhole.com

Home to some of the steepest and most harrowing terrain in the country, Jackson Hole is something of a legend among extreme skiers. Fully 50% of its trails are black or double black diamond, and 10 of them qualify for yellow warning stripes. Those who make it down a total of 100,000 vertical feet in a week become lifelong members of Jackson's "Ski the Big One" challenge and those who top 1,000,000 vertical feet receive a gold belt buckle with their membership. Yet for all the pomp and circumstance surrounding Jackson Hole skiing, the place is about as friendly and unpretentious as your local sledding hill. (Oh, and, did we mention cheap?) This is because winter is actually the off-season here. During the summer, the place is packed solid with tourists setting off for Yellowstone or Grand Tetons National Parks. Not surprisingly, the scaled-down skiing crowd is a piece of cake for locals.

Relax, you don't have to be Olympic-bound to ski the "Hole." It's got a slew of intermediate runs and a good array of gentle slopes for beginners and never-evers. Green-on-the-verge-of-blue-run skiers must be warned, however, Jackson Hole is not an ideal place to make the transition. Its blue runs are harder than those at most resorts and are best for competent intermediates not beginning intermediates. Snowboarders are permitted everywhere at Jackson Hole and have two natural half-pipes to ride as well.

For those more interested in spectacular scenery than killer slopes, cross-country skiing on one of the marked trails in Yellowstone or Grand Tetons is just the thing. There is also a cross-country area called Jackson Hole Nordic Center, located right next to the downhill base.

Jackson Hole is based at Teton Village, 12 miles away from the bigger, bustling town of Jackson. In the village, the Mangy Moose and Beaver Dick's will both start the party with a respectable roar. In town, there are lots of choices (do remember that you're in country music country), including The Million Dollar Cowboy Bar, The Silver Dollar Bar, The Rancher and the Jackson Hole Pub and Brewery. The Southern Teton Area Rapid Transit (START) runs regularly between Teton Village and Jackson until 10 p.m.

California

Lake Tahoe

Whether you are a terrified first-timer or a steep-and-deep machine, Lake Tahoe will accommodate you nicely. With seven major ski areas (and many smaller ones,) including Alpine Meadows, Squaw Valley USA, Northstar-at-Tahoe, Kirkwood, Heavenly, Diamond Peak and Sugar Bowl, that's what it does best. You can usually get access to several areas on a single ticket. Here, we will focus on Alpine Meadows, Squaw Valley and Heavenly, as the others tend to be quieter, family-oriented resorts. (It should be noted that Northstar-at-Tahoe and Kirkwood are a cut above the rest, especially Heavenly, when it comes to never-ever and beginner skiing.)

Heavenly

1-800-243-2836

http://www.skiheavenly.com

Located in the high-energy South Shore area, Heavenly is a massive resort split between California and Nevada. Intermediate and advanced skiers will have a field day here, or more accurately, a field week, with so much interesting terrain to tackle. Beginners and never-evers don't fare so well. First, the maze of trails can be downright confusing. Worse though, most green trails end in an area shot through with fast flyers heading for the lifts. Snowboarders are welcome everywhere at Heavenly. There is a board park on the Nevada side and a half pipe when there is enough snow.

Half of Heavenly's allure is the splashy, flashy night life of the South Shore. In the casino department, there is Ceasar's

Tahoe, Harrah's Lake Tahoe, Harvey's and Horizon's. (If you don't blow a lot of money gambling, their cheap rooms and buffet meals can make your vacation a bargain.) Besides the usual slot machines and blackjack tables, they offer dancing and live music. Other prime picks for the après-ski hours are Carlos Murphy's and the Turtle. Heavenly, as well as several of the casinos, provide free, frequent shuttle bus service between the slopes and the nightlife strip.

Squaw Valley USA
1-800-545-4350
http://www.squaw.com

Squaw Valley, like Vail, is another one of those super-duper, extra-special, something-for-everybody resorts. It first made a name for itself as host of the 1960 Winter Olympics, and kept on moving up from there. With a vast selection of bone-chillingly difficult runs, it has become a mecca for skiing's wunderkind. (Yes, they think quite highly of themselves and they think you should too.) Even so, less-skilled practitioners are not neglected. There is plenty to challenge intermediates, including Olympic High, the same run used for the 1960 men's downhill race. Meanwhile, beginners are afforded the rare chance to practice their turns on top of the mountain instead of the base. Boarders are permitted everywhere at Squaw and also have a terrain park and a half-pipe at their disposal.

If, for some mysterious reason, you get bored schussing or shredding at Squaw, you can always while away the hours swimming, ice-skating or bungee jumping at the High Camp base. For après-ski refreshment, try Bullwhacker's Pub at the Resort at Squaw Creek or the top-rated River Ranch on the Alpine Meadows Access Road. In nearby Tahoe City, Naughty Dawg, Humpty's, Pete'n'Peter's, Rosie's Café or the Pierce Street Annex are good bets. Or, you can truck on up to Truckee and take in some live music at the Bar of America or the Pastime Club, both on Commercial Row. Strike out east and you'll soon hit a clutch of North Lake casinos, including Cal-Neva Lodge and Casino, Hyatt Lake Tahoe, Crystal Bay Club Casino and Tahoe Biltmore Hotel.

To get around the North Lake area catch the Tahoe Area Regional Transit (TART) bus, which runs until 6:30 p.m. on weekdays and 2:30 a.m. on weekends, or the Squaw Valley Free Shuttle.

Alpine Meadows
1-800-441-4423
http://www.skialpine.com/
Perks and amenities might as well be trail names at Alpine Meadows because they probably won't get mentioned any other way. Here, skiing, above all else, is the raison d'être. And it's a pretty darn good reason at that. Intermediate and advanced skiers will love Alpine for its vast collection of interesting and challenging runs. There is also a decent beginners area located in a pleasant low-traffic area. Snowboarders were allowed for the first time during the 1996-97 season. They are permitted everywhere. See Squaw Valley for nightlife and public transportation information. The two are close neighbors.

Part Three   Trail Breaks

Trek Prep

L et's face it, college life can make you want to grab your hiking boots and run headlong into an Ansel Adams photo. At most schools, there simply aren't very many opportunities to get outside, much less into the backcountry. Sure, you dash from your dorm to class and maybe you relax in the quad every once in a while, but there's always something you have to get to next. And if you do get a few minutes to yourself, what are the chances a kindred trail-mate will have a chunk of free time too? What about the chances you can borrow your roommate's car to get there? Where is "there" anyway, and how late is it open?

If it's not a busy schedule that thwarts your outdoor aspirations, it's a load of logistics. But why should you have to cool your outdoor-loving heels for complications like these? Don't know what to do about the time crunch? That's where spring break comes in. It's long enough so that your getting-going time won't cut into your hiking-biking-climbing time. Plus, you and your outdoorsy friends will all be free at the same time. As for logistics, that's where the next two chapters comes in. Here, you'll find information on great springtime destinations, outing clubs, equipment rental and outdoor web resources.

Using Your Outing Club

If you want to go hiking, backpacking, rafting, kayaking, rock climbing or caving this spring break, contact your school's outing club. Many college outing clubs run such trips, welcoming members and non-members alike. Typically, transportation and equipment are provided. Even if your outing club is not running spring break trips, it may be a good place to rent equipment, look at maps or hit up members for sage advice.

Also, find out if your outing club is a member of the Intercollegiate Outing Club Association (IOCA). This student-run group helps link up outing clubs across the country (and Canada) so they can share equipment and plan joint trips. If your outing club is a member, you may be able to join another school's spring break trip or rent out its equipment. IOCA maintains (sometimes) a web site, which lists member schools, details the group's philosophy and provides information on upcoming events: http://www. rpi. edu/dept/union/outing/public/rocmosaic/IOCAmosaic/ IOCA.html.

Where To Rent Equipment

You shouldn't have to bag a camping trip because you don't have the right gear. That doesn't mean you should have to spend hundreds of dollars on brand new equipment either. Instead, look into renting. First, try your outing club. If it doesn't rent or has nothing left, you might try a national retail chain like Eastern Mountain Sports or REI (Recreational Equipment Inc.) Both rent camping equipment, including tents, sleeping bags, sleeping mats, backpacks and camp stoves.

Campground Reservations

If you plan to stay at a campground within a national park during spring break, make reservations. Campgrounds, especially in popular parks like the Grand Canyon and the Everglades, tend to fill up quickly and reserving a site is the only way to ensure you'll have somewhere to sleep when you arrive.

First, call the park to find out which campgrounds accept reservations. Then, reserve your spot as soon as you know your trip dates. In some cases, parks handle campground reservations themselves, but a number, including the Grand Canyon, Everglades, Death Valley and Joshua Tree, use a private reservation service called DESTINET. With DESTINET (1-800-365-2267), you can reserve camp sites about five months in advance.

General Outdoor Web Resources

National Park Service
http://www.nps.gov/
This complete site includes comprehensive descriptions for all national parks. It also gives permit and fee information.

Great Outdoors Recreation Pages (GORP)
http://www.gorp.com/default.htm
Clearly created by denizens of the "Great Outdoors," this aptly acronymed site contains mountains of useful information, including park guides, trail bios, book and media recommendations, gear vendor listings, and dozens of recreation-related web links.

Desert USA
http://www.desertusa.com/
Since desert parks are often most hospitable during March and April, this site is an excellent place to window shop for prospective spring break destinations. In addition to thorough profiles of ten desert parks, it includes fascinating accounts of desert trips and attractions.

U.S. High Points Guide
http://www.inch.com/~dipper/highpoints.html
This site lists each state's highest point. Excelsior! Suddenly, it's clear why Florida will be the first to go when the icecaps melt. Its highest point is only 345 feet above sea level.

Cool Works
http://www.coolworks.com/
Perfect for the soon-to-be-unemployed, this site lists jobs in tons of national parks as well as at camps, ranches and ski resorts.

NINE

Fresh Air Frolics

Weather will and should be your biggest concern when deciding where to "rough it" over spring break. Nothing takes the fun out of camping quicker than frozen sleepless nights, and wet hiking boots. And both are easy to come by in the country's northern backcountry, at least in March. In other words, follow your beach-going friends to the country's toasty southern states.

Florida, Texas, New Mexico, Arizona and California all have beautiful state and national parks that are warm, or on the verge of warm, during spring break season. In this section, we've showcased four major national parks and mentioned several lesser-known national and state parks that fit the warm-weather bill. We've also included two long distance scenic trails, sections of which may be appropriate for spring break hiking and camping.

The Grand Canyon

Although a visit to this natural marvel may seem like a cliché, it's gotta be done. The Grand Canyon is simply too breath-taking to miss. That doesn't mean you have to descend on burro back like the Bradys or take the express lane like Thelma and Louise. In fact, the best way to experience the Grand Canyon is to hike it. Thus, you'll appreciate the immensity of the chasm as only a slow-going, self-powered pedestrian can. Actually, spring break season is a good time to make the requisite pilgrimage because the weather is usually moderate and the crowds are not yet in full throng. (Peak season runs from April through October.)

The Two Rims

Purists (outdoor and otherwise) cannot help but disdain the commercialized and overdeveloped South Rim. A magnet for hotels and tourists, it is rather like a theme park with a fantastic view. While the North Rim is by no means an untouched wilderness, it certainly puts some of the rough back into roughing it. Unfortunately, the roads leading to the North Rim are closed from late October to mid-May due to heavy snowfall. For you spring breakers, this means the South Rim will have to suffice. This does not mean you will be trapped in gift marts and Canyon Burger joints for a week. In fact, once you delve into the inner canyon (under the rim), it won't matter so much what's at the top. (Indeed, you'll probably wonder, at points, if you'll ever make it back to the top.)

Feel Like a Stroll?

Hiking or backpacking in the Grand Canyon can be invigorating, delightful, wearisome or torturous. It all depends on the weather, your experience and your preparation. Temperature-wise, March is an ideal time to go because the temperature in the inner canyon is still moderate, averaging around 71° during the day. (In the heat of summer, inner canyon temperatures can shoot up to 115° or hotter!) Even so, adequate preparation is imperative.

Most hikes into the Canyon entail strenuous descents that can leave campers agonizingly sore the next day. Of course, the ascent back to the rim will be even more trying for out-of-shape hikers. (A handy rule of thumb: A hike to the Colorado River and back up to the South Rim is like climbing the Empire State Building five times.) To make matters worse, hikers often tire quickly because they are not used to the high elevations (The South Rim is about 7000 feet above sea level.). The best way to prepare for the experience is to climb up and down many stairs many times. When it comes to the actual hike, pace yourself and drink plenty of water (a gallon a day per person.)

Getting Below the Rim

There are a number of "corridor trails" that lead to the inner canyon. On the South Rim, the most heavily traveled are the South Kaibab and Bright Angel Trails, both of which descend to the Colorado River. Rangers generally recommend that hikers take the South Kaibab into the Canyon and the less steep Bright Angel back out. The Tonto Trail intersects both South Kaibab and Bright Angel as it crosses the Tonto Platform about 3000 feet below the South Rim (about half way into the Canyon.) On the Canyon floor, the River Trail follows the Colorado River, also intersecting South Kaibab and Bright Angel.

Babbitt's General Store near the South Rim is a good place to rent backpacking and camping equipment. Call in advance to reserve your gear, 520-638-2262.

Grand Canyon Field Institute (GCFI)

Calling all lecture-weary students! How would you like the Grand Canyon to be your classroom? Then think about enrolling in the Grand Canyon Field Institute, which offers classes for hikers, backpackers, naturalists and other outdoors-lovers. Trips range in length from a few days to a few weeks, and in ability level from easy walking to off-trail backpacking. Partnerships with Northern Arizona University and Prescott College allow GCFI to award college credit for some classes. The first trips of the season start in mid-March. For more information:

GCFI
PO Box 399
Grand Canyon, AZ 86023
520-638-2485.

River Trips

If you're thinking about a raft trip down the Colorado River, join the club. Hundreds of people raft it every year, and thanks to the tremendous interest, there are over twenty river trip operators in the Grand Canyon area. Two of the best, according to Outside magazine, are Grand Canyon Dories (209-736-0805) and OARS (209-736-2924). For more information on OARS trips, check out their web site at http://www.oars.com.

Address

Grand Canyon National Park
PO Box 129
Grand Canyon, AZ 86023
(520) 638-7888

Fees

Entrance for private vehicle:	$20
Entrance for cyclist/pedestrian:	$10
Backcountry Permit:	$20
Nightly Impact Fee (per person):	$4

Permits

No permit is required for day hikes below the rim. A Backcountry Permit is required for all overnight stays below the rim. Because these permits, which cost $20, are in such high demand, it's best to reserve them well in advance. Permit requests can be submitted no earlier than the first of the month, four months prior to the start date. For example, for a trip anytime during March 1998, a permit can be requested on or after November 1, 1997. Permit applications can be faxed (520-638-2125) or mailed (postmarked no earlier than the first of the month) to the address above, attention Backcountry Permit Request Form. Keep in mind that small groups (1-6) have a better chance of getting permits than big groups (7-11).

Getting There

The Grand Canyon is located in northwestern Arizona. Its South Rim is about 80 miles northwest of Flagstaff via highway 180. Its North Rim is 44 miles south of Jacob Lake, Arizona via highway 67. Jacob Lake is a small town just south of the Utah border.

Grand Canyon Web Resources

Grand Canyon National Park Homepage
http://www.nps.gov/grca/
Sponsored by the National Park Service, this site includes Grand Canyon facts, fees, phone numbers, addresses, operating hours and other vital statistics.

Grand Canyon National Park
http://www.thecanyon.com/nps
This site is your complete guide to the Canyon. It's got a trip planner, FAQS, trail descriptions, permit rules (and a printable permit request form), Canyon news, directions, weather and a link to the Grand Canyon Field Institute.

The Grand Tour (hosted by GORP)

http://www.gorp.com/gcjunkies/canyon.htm

Created by a cadre of self-proclaimed Canyon Junkies, this site is lighthearted and informative. Besides pictures, a "day-in-the Canyon" profile, and trail info, there is a good list of links to other Canyon sites.

Big Bend

The Talking Heads probably weren't referring to Big Bend, when they sang "We're on the Road to Nowhere," but they could have been. The park is deep in the Chihuahuan Desert of southwest Texas, a hundred miles from the nearest bank or supermarket. Even the first settlers felt its isolation, calling it the "Uninhabited Place." Because it's so remote, Big Bend is among the ten least visited national parks. Its meager tourist population hardly reflects its beauty and grandeur, however. Together, desert, mountain and river make the park visually dramatic and recreationally diverse.

Although Big Bend receives few visitors compared to say, the Grand Canyon, it is fairly crowded during March and April, when the weather is sunny and warm. (Crowded means 800 people. In other words, about one person per 100 acres.) Spring breakers have taken a particular liking to the park and do their part to fill Big Bend's guest books each year.

Mustn't Miss This

- While there's plenty to pique your interest on the desert floor, including havelinas (wild pigs,) scaled quail, prickly pears and giant dagger yucca, it would be a shame to forgo a trip into the Chisos Mountains. Especially notable is the South Rim, which offers some of the most beautiful views in the park. Most hikers opt to take the Laguna Meadow Trail up and the steeper Pinnacles (also called Boot Spring) Trail back down.
- You're sticky, sweaty, tired and achy. You'd cut off your right arm if only a jacuzzi would appear before you in the desert. Well, get out the hacksaw, then head over to Big Bend's hot springs. There, you can soak to your heart's content in a shallow rock basin burbling with 105° spring water. To reach the

hot springs, take the turnoff near Rio Grande Village and follow the dirt road to the hot springs parking lot. The springs are adjacent to the Rio Grande, an easy quarter mile hike from the parking lot.

- Big Bend's location on the Rio Grande makes it easy to hop over to Mexico on impulse. Spend an afternoon in Boquillas, Coahuila, Chihuahua or Santa Elena. Eat a burrito, drink a beer and take a peek inside the local curio shops. Mexican locals will ferry you across the river for a small fee. (Swimming or wading across the muddy waters of the Rio Grande is not suggested.) While such side trips are permitted (no passport required), the U.S. Border Patrol has been known to crack down on crossings to other border towns, including Castolon and Lajitas.

Spring Break Stories: Solo Hiking in Big Bend

During spring break of my senior year, I joined our outing club's backpacking trip to Big Bend National Park in Texas. The 35 hour trip from Oberlin, OH was not too bad except for a severe hailstorm in Dallas, which left my car permanently pock-marked. We pulled into our base camp just after sunrise on the third day, and immediately began exploring.

Our group took two overnight backpacking trips and a number of day trips. The most powerful experience I had was a day trip through a dry riverbed. While the heartier souls had set off on their second overnight trip, my half of the group decided to do some solo exploration. We drove up to the riverbed and split up, each hiker leaving five minutes after the last one had set off. I was the next to last to start. There were no trails, so I just followed the riverbed toward the distant hills. I used desert rock formations as landmarks, hoping I would eventually find my back to the car. I am a person who has great difficulty finding my way around campus, so I was a little nervous about this method of navigation. One large rock seemed to me to evoke a hiker with a backpack, so I figured that as long as I remembered that the hiker was facing the parking area, I would be okay.

The complete solitude I felt hiking along that dry riverbed was both inspiring and frightening. Even though I often hike alone, I am used to frequent reminders that others have been there. In Big Bend you can be only a few hundred yards from another person and still be convinced that you are the only breathing being for miles around. I was afraid I would never get home, yet it was exciting to feel responsible for my own survival. The total peace of the desert tends to bring on revelations unsought.

At one point, I was sitting on the soft silt of the riverbed and saw fellow hiker Justin walking towards me. Initially, I felt relieved and was tempted to ask if I could join him. However, continued solitude was even more compelling than company, so I decided to see how close he would come without noticing me. I sat silently and waited. His footsteps were noiseless in the silt. He came within about 35 yards of me, and then he veered somewhat to the right and followed a different branch of the river. He never saw me, and when I finally stood up about fifteen minutes later, I couldn't see him anymore.

There is one more anecdote from this trip that I feel is worth telling. It happened while our group was camped in the "gravel pit," a group of car campsites near the Rio Grande. A few of us walked down to the beach in the afternoon to see the splendid cliffs of Boquillas, Mexico, on the other side of the river. Unfortunately, I got too close to the water, and my shoes started to sink into the soft mud. I tried to escape, but just wound up sinking deeper and deeper. I finally found myself buried up to my knees, unable to move. Two of my friends took my arms and tried to pull me out, bus as they were each pulling my sideways, in different directions, this was not very effective. Finally, they managed to pull me out by standing in front of me and pulling forward on my arms. My shoes and pants were absolutely caked with mud. In fact, we decided that my shoes were "desert art," and used them to mark our campsite so that returning backpackers could find it.

Overall, Big Bend is a great spring break trip for anyone who is serious about outdoor adventure and has never been to the desert. It is by far the most memorable trip I took while I was in college, and I still get to tell the story every time someone asks me about the hail damage to my car.

Jessica Kagle '95
Oberlin College
Oberlin, OH

Address

Big Bend National Park
PO Box 129
Big Bend National Park, Texas 79834
915-477-2251

Fees

Entrance for private vehicle: $10
Entrance for cyclist/pedestrian: $5

Permits

Big Bend gives out two types of permits for overnight stays, both of which are free. The first type applies to designated sites on park campgrounds, as well as established "primitive" camp sites throughout the park. Because there are a limited number of established camp sites, these permits run out quickly. (The park does not take reservations.) When all sites are filled, advisories are posted at all park entrances. The second type of permit, of which there is an unlimited number, is for general backcountry camping. Permits can be obtained up to 24 hours in advance at any of the park's visitor centers.

Getting There

Take U.S. Route 385 from Marathon, TX to the north entrance, or State Route 118 from Alpine, TX to the west entrance. There are four visitor centers in the park: Persimmon Gap, Panther Junction, Chisos Basin and Rio Grand Village.

Big Bend Web Resources

Big Bend National Park Homepage
http://www.nps.gov/bibe/
Sponsored by the National Park Service, this site includes Big Bend facts, fees, phone numbers, addresses, operating hours and other vital statistics.

Roads and Trails of Big Bend National Park
http://hotx.com/hot/bigbend/bigbendnp/
Contains excellent descriptions of roads and trails, as well as walking and hiking routes in Big Bend. A great resource for the trip-planning phase when you're trying to decide where to go and what you'll have time to cover.

Virtually There: Big Bend
http://www.texasmonthly.com/travel/virtual/bigbend/index.html
Look no further for a thorough and user-friendly guide to Big Bend. This site, maintained by Texas Monthly Magazine, covers everything from the time of day you should arrive to the sights you shouldn't miss.

Death Valley

With uncharacteristic verve, the National Park Service exclaims about Death Valley, "Allow one full lifetime to explore all of this huge desert park." They aren't kidding. It's the largest national park in the continental United States with literally millions of acres to explore. One minute, it's a vast wasteland of rock and sand, the next, it's a palette in flux, reflecting panes of gold, red, orange and purple. No surprise really, that parts of *Return of the Jedi* were filmed here.

Don't be put off by the park's harrowing name. It's not a cryptic warning, just a historical artifact from the days when gold rushers perished here while in transit to boom towns farther west. Of course, those unfortunate souls didn't have the luxury of spring break, so they trekked through in the summer when temperatures soared. (In 1913, the mercury hit a record high of 134°.)

Desert Rat Rambles
In the "breathtaking vista" department, Dante's View, accessible by car, is particularly impressive. If you'd rather sweat it out for such visual feasts, tackle the Wildrose Peak or Telescope Peak Trails. Both yield panoramic views of Death Valley, not to mention interesting scenery on the way up. Telescope Peak is the highest point in the park at 11,049 feet. Also, a trip to Death Valley is simply not complete without a frolic on the sand dunes. The Death Valley Dunes are the easiest to visit, accessible from Highway 190. The Eureka Dunes are also reasonably accessible in good weather.

If you've been wanting to treat your mountain bike to something a little rougher than campus sidewalks, bring it to Death Valley with you. While bikers are barred from trails, they are permitted on any of the park's dirt and paved roads. Consider a ride on Artist's Drive, Titus Canyon Road or Trail Canyon Road.

Serious cyclists might want to consider entering the Death Valley Century ride, held in March around the time of a full moon. Hugh Murphy Productions organizes the ride, in addition to several other western cycling events. For information, write:

Hugh Murphy Productions
2364 Mountain Brook Dr.
Hacienda Heights, CA 91745
e-mail: HUGHMURPHY@bbcnet.com

Address

Death Valley National Park
PO Box 579
Death Valley, CA 92328
760-786-2231

Fees

Entrance for private vehicle: $10
Entrance for cyclist/pedestrian: $5

Permits

Permits are not required for backcountry camping, however, visitors are strongly encouraged to fill out a Backcountry Registration Form before they set out. These forms are available at the Visitor Center or any Ranger Station. Backcountry camping is not permitted on the valley floor from Ashord Mill to 5 miles north of Stovepipe Wells. Visitors may car camp along most primitive dirt roads in Death Valley, though not along maintained dirt roads or paved roads. Again, no permit is necessary.

Getting There

Death Valley is on south-central California's eastern border, 120 miles northwest of Las Vegas and 300 miles northeast of Los Angeles. Take either California Route 178 or 190 into the park's western entrances. Both are accessible from U.S. Route 395. To enter the park from the east, take Nevada Route 267, 373 or 374. All are accessible from U.S. Route 95.

Death Valley Web Resources

Death Valley National Park Homepage
http://www.nps.gov/deva/
Sponsored by the National Park Service, this site includes Death Valley facts, fees, phone numbers, addresses, operating hours and other vital statistics.

Death Valley National Park
http://www.desertusa.com/dv/du_dvpmain.html
This site, maintained by Desert USA (see General Outdoor Web Resources in Chapter 8) is a complete guide to Death Valley. In addition to a great physical description of the park, you get the full story on trails, camping and logistics.

Death Valley by Eastern Sierra Lovers
http://www.mammothweb.com/sierraweb/sightseeing/deathvalley/default.html
This is one of a dozen well-crafted sites created by people who think the Eastern Sierra Nevada Mountains are about the niftiest place on earth. In addition to a good list of park features, trails, roads and camp grounds, there is a first-rate (and fast-loading) photo gallery.

The Everglades

In 1840, the state of Florida pronounced the Everglades region "wholly valueless" and asked the federal government to help pay for its drainage. Somehow, the Everglades, situated at Florida's southern tip, fought its way back from ignominy and today carries a string of honorable designations, including International Biosphere Reserve, Wetland of International Significance and National Wilderness Area. In short, the state realized that just because the Everglades couldn't be farmed, didn't mean it wasn't worth keeping. (That said, creeping development and polluting sugar-growers now pose a serious threat to the Glades.)

If you haven't been to the Everglades, you've probably never seen anything like it. Essentially, it is a river fifty miles wide, only inches deep in some spots, coursing slowly south until it empties into Florida Bay. (Only the southern tip of this river is actually protected by the national park.) Along with thousands of plant species, the Everglades' wetland environment sustains hundreds of animal species, making it one of the best parks in the country for wildlife-watching. Visitors routinely spot alligators, turtles, snakes, wood storks, egrets, osprey and great blue herons.

Winter, which runs from about December through April, is the dry season in the Everglades, and the best time to visit. Summertime, on the other hand, is the wet season, a glorious time of 90° heat, 90% humidity, torrential downpours and fierce mosquito militias.

Mosquito Coast

When park guides list "mosquito-free" excursions, you know it's time to take these pests seriously. Such is the case with the Everglades, which, by dint of its swampy environs, plays host to some of North America's wildest mosquito breed-ins. If you'd rather not get eaten alive, use plenty of insect repellent. If you're allergic to repellent or just absentminded, expect to emerge from your trip with bites on bites on bites.

Marsh Madness

The best way to see the Everglades is to get right down in the middle of things. If you feel uncomfortable riding alligator-back, there's always canoeing or kayaking. Canoe trails abound in the park, particularly around the Flamingo and Gulf Coast areas. Ultra-ambitious paddlers might enjoy a trip down the 99-mile Wilderness Waterway, which connects Flamingo and Everglades City. The one-way trip takes between 8 and 10 days. Canoe rentals are available at Flamingo Marina, Gulf Coast Visitor Center and in Everglades City. There is a boat launch fee of $3.

Surprisingly, biking is also a popular way to see the Everglades. If you're hoping to see wildlife, the 15 mile Shark Valley Loop Road is a good choice, as alligators, snakes, turtles and otters all live in the vicinity. Bicycle rentals are available at Flamingo Marina and Shark Valley Visitor Center.

Address
Everglades National Park
40001 State Road 9336
Homestead, FL 33034-6733
305-242-7700

Fees
Entrance for private vehicle: $10
Entrance for pedestrian/cyclist: $5

Permits
Permits are required for all overnight stays in the Everglades backcountry. They cost $10 for groups of 1 to 6 and $20 for groups of 7 to 12. All but a few backcountry camp sites are accessible only by canoe or boat.

Getting There
Main Entrance: From all points north, take the Florida Turnpike (Route 821) south to the Florida City exit. Turn right onto Palm Drive at the first traffic light and follow the signs to the entrance.

Shark Valley Visitor Center: Take the Florida Turnpike south to U.S. Route 41 (also called the Tamiami Trail). Go west 25 miles on 41 following signs to Shark Valley.

Gulf Coast Visitor Center: Take Route 41 east. At the junction of U.S. Route 29, go south to Everglades City, then follow the signs to the park entrance.

Everglades Web Resources
Everglades National Park Page
http://www.nps.gov/ever/
Sponsored by the National Park Service, this site includes Everglades facts, fees, phone numbers, addresses, operating hours and other vital statistics.

Everglades by the American Park Network
http://www.americanparknetwork.com/parkinfo/ev/aag/glance.html
Both practical and educational, this site provides camping, hiking and activity information, as well as profiles of park geology and wildlife.

Other National Parks

Joshua Tree National Park (CA)
619-367-7511
http://www.nps.gov/jotr/
Located about 140 miles east of Los Angeles, this park gets its name from the unique trees that congregate in its higher, wetter Mojave Desert half. In recent years, Joshua Tree has become well known as an excellent rock-climbing venue. Mountain biking is also popular here.

Petrified Forest National Park (AZ)
602-524-6228
http://www.nps.gov/pefo/
A showcase for life that once was, this park features petrified trees, Indian ruins and parts of the colorful Painted Desert. As there are few marked or established trails in the park, hiking in the backcountry requires an acute sense of direction or a compass and a topographical map. It's perfect for orienteers. The park is located in northwestern Arizona.

State Parks

Slide Rock State Park (AZ)
520-282-3034
This little 43 acre park, just North of Sedona, Arizona, features a 30-foot long water slide worn into the Oak Creek bed. After you've taken full advantage of this natural playground, take a hike among the red rocks and pine forests of Oak Creek Canyon. The park closes at night, but there are several Forest Service campgrounds nearby.

John Pennecamp Coral Reef State Park (FL)
305-451-1202
The heart and soul of this stunning north Florida Keys park is its coral reef. Thus, come prepared to go snorkeling or scuba diving. You'll see colorful fish, exotic sea creatures and, of course, lots of coral. If you're lucky, you'll run into a nine-foot algae-covered Christ. The bronze statue was sunk a few years back as a memorial to dead sailors. The park closes at night, but there are campgrounds close by.

Bahia Honda State Recreation Area (FL)
305-872-2353
Located in the middle Florida Keys, about 20 miles west of Marathon, this beautiful park has a lot to offer those who are looking for a cross between a beach break and a camping trip. Swim in Bahia Honda's lagoons, Camp on its sandy beaches, hike into its dense tropical forest, windsurf on its bay or snorkel and scuba dive in its coral reefs.

Long Distance Scenic Trails

Appalachian National Scenic Trail (2159 miles)
304-535-6331
http://www.fred.net/kathy/at.html
This famous hiking trail extends from Mount Katahdin in Maine to Springer Mountain in Georgia along the crest of the Appalachian Mountains. Although even its southern extremities are bound to be rather cool (between 55° and 65° during the day and 30° to 40° at night) during spring break, the AT is a charmer and will probably win you over, cold fingers and all.

Pacific Crest National Scenic Trail (2638 miles)
916-349-2109
http://www.gorp.com/pcta/
This long distance footpath is the West's version of the Appalachian Trail, passing from Canada to Mexico via Washington, Oregon and California. The 406 mile Desert Crest part of the trail, which extends from Tenachapi Pass (near Bakersfield, CA) to the California border town of Campo, is probably temperate enough for March-time trips.

Part Four   Spring Break Alternatives

Alternative Spring Break

TEN

> *Never doubt that a small group of thoughtful concerned citizens can change the world; indeed, it's the only thing that ever has.*
>
> —*Margaret Mead*

From ice-fishing in Minnesota to yachting in the Bimini Islands, students have always managed to think up creative alternatives to the Florida spring break sojourn. Still, the folks who really put the "alternative" into "Alternative Spring Break" (ASB) are the ones who pioneered the service trip. Yep, that's the one where students spend a week building houses for low-income families, repairing trails, serving meals to homeless people, helping out in AIDS clinics, tutoring Head-Start children, working on Indian reservations, rescuing animals affected by oil spills or participating in some other community service projects.

Why Would I Want to Do an ASB?

Students of the traditional beach break persuasion might ask, "Why Alternative Spring Break? Isn't that like wanting an alternative to winning the lottery? But for an increasing number of students, the week long booze-fest isn't all it's cracked up to be. There are sunburns and hangovers to contend with, but worse, the whole affair tends to feel superficial after awhile. Many students would rather spend their vacation week doing something useful and rewarding, and alternative breaks are exactly that.

They are also the best antidote to that insidious college mentality that's got you believing that life's most pressing problems are lost lecture notes and overlapping extracurricular activities. Sure, in the back of your mind, you know there are more serious problems in the world, but often, it doesn't register until you hop in the "trenches" and see them first hand. For those who are too

busy to volunteer during the semester, ASBs are the perfect vehicle for a sustained and meaningful service effort.

ASB's Infancy

The first Alternative Spring Breaks popped up in the mid-eighties
when spring breakers were beginning to branch out from the
beach. Most schools started out with only one or two trips, usually to local sites. In 1991, two enterprising graduates of Vanderbilt University in Nashville, Tennessee decided Alternative Spring
Break needed an agent, somebody to encourage it, promote it and
represent it. They filled the position by forming a non-profit called
Breakaway: the Alternative Break Connection. Based at Vanderbilt, Breakaway developed a series of workshops, trainings and
manuals to assist Alternative Spring Break organizers.

By the mid-nineties, a number of schools had begun to offer
multiple trips, a few even to international destinations. Some
schools established full-time ASB clubs, others expanded their
programs by partnering with other colleges and universities. Professors got into the act as well, developing quarter and semes-
ter-length classes around ASB projects. Today, ASB trips are in
such high demand at some schools that dozens of applicants are
turned away each year. All told, over 15,000 students participated
in 350 ASB projects during spring break '97.

The ASB Experience

In some ways, ASB trips aren't all that different from non-ASB
trips. Either way, at some point, you'll find yourself cruising down
the highway at 3 a.m., foraging for chips and singing "Hey-ey
take the money and run." You'll also find that you have a love-
hate relationship with your companions. One minute you'll think,
"I love this guy!" The next you'll scream, "Man, why can't you
just pump the frickin' gas?" Often, you'll forge bonds unlike any
you've experienced at school. After all, you'll spend entire days
along side each other, painting, building, cleaning and
schlepping. You'll eat your bag lunches, church dinners and do-
nated meals together, and at night you'll all crash in church halls,
dormitories or YMCA rooms.

Volunteers Wanted, No Droids

Remember, Alternative Spring Breaker is not synonymous with volunteer robot. You are not expected to put your nose to the grindstone and keep it there for a week. At most ASB sites, college students are a strange, but welcome breed. You may get a cold glance now and then, but most people will gladly tell you their stories and talk with you about the problems the ASB is trying to address.

Spirng Break Stories: Seeing Homelessness in a Different Light

In Washington, DC, we volunteered at the Community for Creative Non-Violence (a homeless shelter where we also stayed), Bread for the City/Zaccheus Clinic (an organization that distributes free food and provides medical services to the homeless), a women's shelter and Martha's Table (provides meals for the homeless). We prepared food, sorted clothing and talked to the people receiving these services. After meeting so many homeless people, and hearing them tell their stories, I realized it could happen to anyone.

For me, the best experiences came from talking to the people. I met people from all walks of life, some who actually had college educations and were living pretty well until something happened to them (drug abuse, job loss, domestic violence). One of the people I met was a practicing attorney, who was living at the shelter because her spouse was physically abusive. Like many of the people I met, she was trying to put her life back together.

The trip was a big wake-up call for me. Being from Miami, I see homeless people all the time. Until I came on the ASB, I always thought of the homeless as the ones with drug problems, which was a very narrow view of reality. In DC, I challenged this stereotype and opened my eyes to a problem that is much more complicated than I realized.

Milena Garcia '97
University of Miami
Miami, FL

It Works Both Ways

While you will certainly learn from the individuals you encounter during alternative break, you may also be a mentor and role model in your own right. The ASB students of Virginia Technical University are a case in point. Six years ago, they began coming to Ivanhoe, Virginia for spring break. They repaired buildings, installed bathrooms and cleared brush lots in this impoverished former mining town. Probably most significant, however, was their impact on Ivanhoe's youth. Before Virginia Tech's ASB program began, 75% of the town's teens dropped out of high school. Under the circumstances, the statistics were not surprising. Ivanhoe was a run-down town with few good jobs and even fewer success stories. College wasn't even a blip on the screen for most kids.

During their visits, ASB students chatted with local kids about future possibilities, and even broached the subject of college. For many teens, it was the first time they'd heard peers speak highly of school. And if the words weren't convincing, the college students themselves were proof of education's perks: independence, wealth (comparatively) and a can-do attitude. Gradually, things changed in Ivanhoe. Today, high school drop-outs are rare and some natives even go on to college.

Building a Better Activist

Although students generally emerge from the ASB experience with a new appreciation for whatever social or environmental problem they tackled, few understand the political and economic realities that go along with it. To this end, many ASB organizers incorporate issue-education into their trips. This can involve everything from meetings with government officials and national activists to reading assignments and group discussions. These opportunities help students understand the scope and complexity of the problems they are taking on. As a result, many students return to their service activities with a unique perspective on their role and potential as social activists.

One ASB group from the University of Michigan prepared for their work in a Washington, DC soup kitchen by reading *Diary of a Homeless Man* and listening to a National Public Radio series on homelessness. While in DC, they supplemented their service with a visit to the Department of Housing and Urban Development (HUD), the National Coalition on Homelessness and a law firm working on homelessness issues. At these meetings, they learned about the causes of homelessness, the severity of the problem in DC, how the local shelter system works and what both the federal government and the private sector are doing to remedy the problem.

Curriculum-Based Alternative Breaks (CBAB)

As informative as alternative breaks can be, there's only so much students can really learn about an acute social problem in a week. Thus, in the past several years, some colleges and universities have begun experimenting with service-learning courses that incorporate ASB trips. These are called Curriculum-Based Alternative Breaks and require students to spend a semester (sometimes less) in the classroom learning about the social problem they will confront on spring break. Often, because of the cross-disciplinary nature of issues like poverty or pollution, professors from different departments team teach the classes, which are typically worth two or three credits.

Michigan's Model

At the University of Michigan, professors of Economics, Sociology and Psychology joined forces last year to teach a seminar examining poverty in Detroit. Below is a basic version of their syllabus and reading list:

Class 1:   Why is There Poverty?
Reading: *Lives on the Boundary.* Mike Rose
            Rachel and Her Children. Jonathan Kozol
            *Two Nations: Black and White, Separate, Hostile,
            Unequal.* Andrew Hacker

Class 2:   An Economic Perspective on Poverty
Reading: *America Unequal.* Sheldon Danziger
            and Peter Gottschalk

Class 3:   Community Organizing in Detroit in the 1970s
Reading: *Detroit: City of Race, Class and Violence.*
            B.J. Widick

Class 4:   Health Care in Detroit
Reading: *The Health of the African American
            Population.* David R. Williams
            *Origins and Destinies: Immigration, Race and
            Ethnicity in America.* S. Pedraza and R.G. Rumbaut

Class 5:   Approaches to Community Organizing in
              Detroit (led by a panel of community activists)

Class 6:   Psychological Dimensions of the Community
              Service Experience
Reading: *The Uncommitted: Alienated Youth in
              American Society.* Kenneth Keniston

Class 7:   What We Have Learned from the Service
              Projects

Class 8:   Multimedia Presentations by Class Members

Spring Break Stories: Definitely Not a Week at Home

While most of my friends ventured to warm, exotic places for their
spring break, I found myself in the cold and frigid state of Maine.
There, my ASB group and I worked at a co-op called H.O.M.E. (Home
Owners united for More Employment), a small community whose
purpose is to help people earn a living on their own. Mainly, H.O.M.E.
builds low-income housing, but it also operates a wood shop, a general store, a school and a weaving shop.

The living accommodations were not exactly luxurious. To give
you an idea, picture twenty college students camped out in your living room. Kind of tight, but we survived. We were allowed to take
only one shower the entire week so you can imagine that after three
days some of us were smelling a little ripe. In that large room we
learned a lot about each other and life. Strangers became friends and
friends became even closer.

The second day, a friend and I were asked to help pull Hank's
(the co-op cook) car from his driveway because it had skidded off
to the side. We didn't realize the driveway was really a four mile
road up the side of a mountain. Assisting one of the co-op's workers, an American Indian named Mike, we spent the entire morning
throwing gravel onto this icy dirt road. While we worked, Mike told
us stories about his tribe and his people. We just worked and
laughed the whole time, and, in the end, rescued the cook from his
high terrain.

Jason Re '99
St. Anselm College
Manchester, New Hampshire

A Stand-Out Host Organization

Habitat For Humanity

While hundreds of non-profit organizations invite ASB students to volunteer each year, Habitat for Humanity, which builds houses for low-income families, leads the pack. In 1997, more than 6000 students, or over one third of alternative breakers, worked on Habitat houses during spring break. Habitat, a non-denominational Christian organization, has been so successful with its ASB program because it offers a large number of work sites and runs a tight ship.

Most importantly, Collegiate Challenge, the arm of Habitat that organizes ASB building trips, has made the student organizer's job easy. To pick a site, students simply peruse a detailed site directory, listing locations, costs, available dates and regional highlights. During the actual trip, Habitat representatives report to each site to work alongside students and coordinate lodging and other logistics. Collegiate Challenge's spring break project season runs from mid-February to early April, which means that up to seven colleges may work on the same house in less than two months. Considering that non-ASB building typically occurs only on weekends, ASB trips are highly productive. Houses often move from framing to roofing in less than a month.

For most Collegiate Challenge trips, ASB participants pay an affiliate contribution to the local chapter sponsoring the project. This fee usually ranges from $75 to $150 per person. The contribution covers the cost of building materials and accommodations for the week. Students must pay for transportation and food themselves (lunch is often provided by local Habitat volunteers). In addition to the affiliate contribution, students must pay a $10 per-person program fee. Collegiate Challenge officials recommend that ASB groups make reservations three or more months in advance of their break. For more information, contact:

Habitat For Humanity International
Collegiate Challenge
Campus Chapters and Youth Programs
121 Habitat Street
Americus, GA 31709-3498
912-924-6935, x 200, 215, 410
web address: http://www.habitat.org

Stand-Out ASB Clubs

Vanderbilt University
Nashville, TN
http://osiris.vuse.vanderbilt.edu/asb/asb.htm
Home to Break Away, it's no surprise that Vanderbilt University has produced an exemplary Alternative Spring Break program. In March 1997, 314 students worked on 23 ASB projects, four of which are profiled below.

- Although they never left town, one Vanderbilt group worked on a particularly unusual ASB project. Cooperating with a local chapter of the United Cerebral Palsy Association (UCPA), ASB participants built wheelchair ramps for low-income people with disabilities during the day. At night, they played wheelchair basketball and other sports with those attending UCPA events.
- Another dozen students traveled to Daufuskie, South Carolina, to work with the last remaining Gullah community. While students tutored local children and helped clean up the island, they learned about the Gullah, who are descendants of slaves and have retained a rich African heritage.
- Finally, Vanderbilt sponsored trips to Monterrey, Mexico and Lima, Peru, where the majority of citizens live in poverty. Through local aid organizations, ASB participants worked directly with the poor, providing them food and medical services. For both trips, students were expected to have a working knowledge of Spanish.

Vanderbilt's ASB club is also one of the few to offer need-based scholarships for its trips.

Stanford University
Palo Alto, CA
http://www.stanford.edu
Last year, Stanford's Alternative Spring Break Club won Break Away's Outstanding Program of the Year award. The honor went to Stanford's ASB club because of its innovative approach to funding and publicity. In 1996, the club asked students to vote to increase Stanford's student activity fee by $1.45 per person to support Alternative Spring Break initiatives. The proposal passed in

a school-wide referendum, channeling an additional $9208 to the club each year.

The new capital helped Stanford add three new trips to its ASB program, covering women's issues, children's issues and environmental policy. Stanford now offers a total of eleven trips, four of which incorporate 2-credit winter term courses. Also in 1996, Stanford students won a separate grant from the Provost to videotape their ASB trip to Los Angeles, where they worked with homeless people. The group subsequently showed the video around campus to raise student awareness about homelessness and encourage campus activism.

University of Michigan
Ann Arbor, MI
http://www.umich.edu/~ocsl/asb/index.html
As a big school with a big reputation, a big research center and a big-time football team, it's no surprise that the University of Michigan has one of the biggest Alternative Spring Break programs around. In 1990, when Michigan's ASB program began, participants worked with Habitat for Humanity at two local sites. Today, participants have 32 projects to choose from, ranging from assisting Haitian refugees in Miami to working at the Madison Square Boys and Girls Club in New York City.

Michigan's ASB club is particularly effective because it has a comprehensive leadership structure. Five teams, including Fundraising and Finance; Site Development; Reflection, Education and Training; Public Relations; and Special Projects, run the program. The club is currently working to establish a service immersion day in the fall and a full-scale Alternative Summer Break program.

Finding or Starting an ASB Program

While Alternative Spring Break can safely be classified as a movement, it is a slow, creeping one. In fact, schools with ASB clubs are the exception, not the rule. So how can you do an Alternative Spring Break if your school doesn't have an ASB club? The easiest way is to sign on with a non-profit organization that sponsors its own ASB program. The following organizations operate alternative spring break programs open to individuals.

Oxfam America

1-800-597-FAST

http://www.charity.org/oxfam.html

This social justice organization has operated an Alternative Spring Break program for high school and college students since 1996. While service is always involved, the emphasis is on issue education. In the program's first year, participants traveled to El Salvador to build a house and help locals with their coffee crop. In 1997, one group of about 20 worked with migrant farm workers in Florida and a second smaller group worked with indigenous people of the rain forest in Bolivia. Trips to California and Senegal, West Africa are tentatively set for spring break '98. Domestic trips cost around $500, airfare included. International trips cost around $1500, airfare included. Partial scholarships are available. Interested students should call Oxfam America to request information and an ASB application. Applications are due in early January.

Christmas in April

1-800-473-4229

http://www.pdi.com/cina-usa/index.html

This national organization works to rehabilitate the houses of low-income homeowners, particularly the elderly and people with disabilities. Each year, around 200 students participate in Christmas in April's ASB program, which began in 1995. Typically, students help renovate homes, though in 1997, they took part in a special initiative called Spring Rebuild, in which they rebuilt churches in Virginia, Tennessee and Florida. The churches had been burned down by arsonists in 1995 and 1996. Christmas in April's ASB program runs for three weeks in March and costs a minimum of $100 per person (not including transportation). While students must fill out a short application, they are actually chosen on a first-come, first-served basis. Christmas in April is not affiliated with any religion or faith.

Habitat For Humanity

912-924-6935, x 200, 215, 410

http://www.habitat.org

Habitat is best equipped to work with student groups, though it does accept individual spring break volunteers. These students are generally placed with adult volunteers, not with other college groups. If you'd like to work with Habitat in this capacity, you'll probably be happiest if you enlist a friend or two. This way you can split transportation costs and you'll have some company.

Linking Up With Other Schools

Occasionally, students at schools with no ASB programs manage to do spring break service projects by linking up with schools that do run ASB trips. In theory, it's an ideal solution. In practice, it's often a complicated proposition. First, with many schools turning away their own students for ASB spots, few have space for outside applicants. Even schools that do have room for outsiders may not accept them because of liability issues. Usually, it's because the school's insurance will not cover outside students.

Organizing Your Own ASB Trip

Look around! Somewhere out there is an Alternative Spring Break group waiting to be formed. Consider your soccer team, your sorority, your church group or a just a bunch of friends. Once you've got a group of interested students together, it's time to find a project. You'll probably have the best luck working with an organization like Habitat for Humanity, which has a well-established spring break program.

If you'd rather work with another organization or tackle a different issue, try calling local non-profits. If they don't have any service projects for you, they may be able to refer you to an agency that does. You might also talk to professors about volunteering opportunities. They may be working on an interesting academic project that involves community service or requires volunteer help. Take, for example, the environmental studies professor who's organizing a creek clean-up or the art professor who's bringing pottery into local nursing homes.

Most volunteer-fueled organizations cannot help but go gaga at the prospect of getting a full-time work crew for a week. Unfortunately, if the organization or project is small, disorganized or simply unaccustomed to receiving much volunteer help, students might be left with a lot of dead time during the trip. Before you commit to a project, make sure it can accommodate your numbers and keep your group busy throughout the week. Also, make sure there will be variety in your work. If you end up painting baseboards for five days, you're liable to contract a bad case of ennui. Another thing to remember when organizing your own ASB, is to leave yourself plenty of lead time. This means months, not weeks. Between recruiting a group and finding a compatible project, you'll need every minute.

Spring Break Stories: Swamp Tales

Since 1996, Alternative Spring Break students have journeyed to Louisiana to help Michael Greene, a professor of Biology at Southeastern Louisiana University, work on a massive swamp restoration project. In 1997, students from Vanderbilt University, the University of Miami and East Oregon State participated. Professor Greene provided the following account of an average day in swamp restoration land.

Roll 'em out of their bunks at 6:30 or 7 a.m., breakfast, and ready to go by 8:00 a.m. Stuff an apple or banana into knapsacks and head to the planting site in canoes. The students stapled protective mats to the ground, planted saplings and placed protective sleeves around the trees. They mostly worked in pairs, with several pairs specializing in a particular task. This would often stimulate a delightful competitive bantering between the various "unions." "Matters are the best!" "Tubers are the most creative!" "Y'all would be nothing without the Planting union!" (This also boosted productivity greatly!)

I stayed with them at the field station and worked side by side with them every day. While they gained sufficient knowledge to continue on their own after a few hours, they did have questions about the ecology of the area and sometimes needed a guiding hand also. We either worked until early to mid afternoon and knocked off after lunch, or broke around noon and went back to work until about 3 p.m. When we worked half days, many students spent their free time exploring the wetlands in canoes. (After all, learning plays a big role in ASB activities—at least it does in mine!)

We put students up at Turtle Cove (accessible only by boat) and they brought their own food. Their meals were as varied as they were. Some had Spam and mac 'n cheese dinners frequently. Others took pride in cooking meals reflecting their cultural heritage. Nighttime activities ranged from sleep (flat wore those suckers out!) to alligator and nutria "hunts" using flashlights and spotlights. Students also played cards, charades, made-up games and looked at aquatic organisms under microscopes.

As I worked with the students, I saw their confidence and self-assurance grow and mature as they learned about wetlands and began to appreciate the subtle connections abundant in such an environment. The swamp will take much longer to revive than it did to destroy, but we have a vision and are working toward that vision. There is no doubt that this Alternative Break project was a good idea and I will continue to do it as long as I am able.

Getting to Know Breakaway

As mentioned before, Break Away was created to advance the alternative break movement by helping students become strong leaders and develop successful ASB programs. Besides offering several trainings and manuals on building alternative break programs, Break Away runs a Campus Chapters program. Member schools can use the Break Away name and logo, and receive discounts on Break Away products. Membership is $125 the first year and $75 to renew. Break Away also gives out three annual awards for excellence in the alternative break field. These include Alternative Break Program of the Year, Host Agency of the Year and Curriculum-Based Alternative Break of the Year.

Break Away Trainings

Alternative Break Citizenship Schools (ABCs)

A week-long summertime seminar to teach students how to start or enhance a multi-site ASB program. There are workshops, speakers and discussions, plus a service project.
    Cost: $260 per participant, covers food, lodging and materials.
    Location: Nashville only

Site Leader Retreats

Weekend trainings to help site leaders learn techniques of group-building and facilitation and develop educational supplements and post-break programming.
    Cost: Undetermined, will probably range from $300-$600.
    Location: Training sites across the country

National Conference

Every year, Breakaway holds a national conference in which its member chapters come together for the usual assortment of convention activities: workshops, social events and awards. Attendees also do a community service project.

Break Away hires one intern each year to organize its national conference. The position, which is paid, runs from June through December.

Cost: Probably between $80 and $100
Location: University of Michigan in Ann Arbor in '97
Dates: November 7-9, 1997

Special Grants

These are, in a word, scholarships. They are available to Alternative Break Citizenship (ABC) School or National Conference participants. Grant applications are available in January for the ABC School and August for the National Conference. Special grants are also available to new or particularly innovative ASB programs seeking Break Away Chapter membership.

BREAK AWAY PUBLICATIONS

The SiteBank Catalog

A directory of volunteer sites across the country. This publication is also available on Break Away's web site.
Cost: $20 postpaid

Break Away: Organizing an Alternative Spring Break

A 90-page guide to starting an Alternative Break program. This manual covers such topics as financing, selecting program leaders and participants, and finding a site.
Cost: $12 postpaid

Site Leader Survival Manual

A guide for ASB site leaders covering conflict resolution, facilitation, reflection and group-building.
Cost: $17 postpaid

Curriculum Based Alternative Break: the Manual

This guide will help students, faculty and staff incorporate ASB trips into college classes on related issues.
Cost: $12 postpaid

Break Away
6026 Station B
Nashville, TN 37235
(615) 343-0385
e-mail: BRAKAWAY@ctrvax.Vanderbilt.edu
web: http://www.vanderbilt.edu/breakaway

Web Resources for Volunteers and Social Activists

Who Cares? A Journal of Service and Action
http://www.whocares.org/
Produced quarterly, this magazine features news about community service as well as profiles of activists and innovative service programs. For all of you promising writers out there, check out Who Cares' submission guidelines. The site also includes a database of national service organizations.

COOL (Campus Outreach Opportunity League)
http://www.cool2serve.org
Tailored to college students, this group provides a directory of national and regional service organizations. Students working to promote community service at school or stir up interest in an upstart ASB program might look into COOL's "Into the Streets" program (slogan: *Try it for a day, you may love it for a lifetime*).

SERVEnet
http://www.servenet.org/
Service-minded students should bookmark this site, which besides the usual database of volunteer organizations, has several valuable features. Users can tap into a list of local volunteer opportunities by entering their zip code. They can also peruse SERVEnet's calendar of events, which lists upcoming conferences, retreats and workshops dealing with community service and social activism. Unemployed do-gooders will love the Career Center, which lists community service-related job openings (both nonprofit and for-profit) across the country.

ELEVEN

I Still Haven't Found
What I'm Looking For

Doing Europe

If you're studying in Europe or Britain for a year or semester, don't even think of going home over spring break. Instead, strap on a backpack, buy a rail pass and let your wanderlust take over. You ought not need convincing, but if you're on the fence, consider these factors:

- Who knows if you'll ever be back. Even if you do return one day, will you be young and frisky enough to carry a pack, chase down trains, crash in hostels and subsist on bread and cheese? Carpe Diem.
- If you budget carefully, it won't cost you much more to see Europe than it would to fly back to the States for break. In fact, many student travelers scrape by on $40 a day or less.
- What are international friends for? Showing you around their hometowns of course! Why not visit your European classmates over spring break and get a local's perspective on things? Offer to return the favor when they come to the States.
- Spring is a good time to see Europe, especially Mediterranean Europe, because the weather should be warming up. This year, why not see how the beaches of Greece measure up to good old Daytona?

Good Guides

As a low-budget backpacker, the last thing you need is a Fielding or Michelin guide recommending blue-ribbon restaurants and five-star hotels. You need to know which hostels have late check-in, where you can buy cheap sandwich fixings and what day the museums are free. The following guides all cater to the shoestring explorer.

Let's Go Guides
1-800-5-LETSGO
http://hsa.net/travel
These ubiquitous yellow guides, written by Harvard students, are the original budget traveler's Bible. They've been around since the sixties and are consistently candid and informative.

Berkeley Guides
http://www.fodors.com
These guides are UC Berkeley's answer to *Let's Go*. They are also written by students and adopt a similar witty, matter-of-fact tone. A little more "granola" than *Let's Go*, the Berkeley Guides put greater emphasis on outdoor excursions and interaction with locals.

Lonely Planet Guides
http://www.lonelyplanet.com
The Lonely Planet "On a Shoestring" line is perfect for the low-budget backpacker. LP books are extremely thorough and often focus on off-the-beaten path attractions.

Picking a Pass
When it comes to getting around in Britain and Europe, rail travel is the way to go. (See the anecdote below for proof.) Trains go almost everywhere and are relatively inexpensive. If you plan to spend your break country-hopping, consider buying a rail pass. These allow holders unlimited train travel in Europe or Britain for a certain period, usually three or four weeks.

Eurail Youthpass
http://www.eurail.com/
This is the rail pass you'll find in the money belts of most American students. It is available to non-Europeans under 26 and is good for unlimited second-class train travel in 17 Western European countries and Ireland. The 15 day pass costs $365, the 21 day pass costs $475 and the one month pass costs $587. Those with lighter travel schedules might be better off with a Flexipass, which entitles the holder to a set number of travel days within a certain period. For example, 8 days per month. The cost is $431 for 10 days per 2 months and $568 for 15 days per 2 months. Eurail

passes must be purchased in the U.S., so make sure you buy yours before you leave.

BritRail Youth Pass
http://www.eurail.com/britrail/
This works just like the Eurail pass except it covers England, Scotland and Wales. A 15 day pass costs $305, a 22 day pass costs $389 and a 1 month pass costs $450. BritRail also offers Flexipasses. The cost is $245 for 8 days per month and $365 for 15 days per two months.

InterRail Youth Pass

These passes are available to Europeans, or foreigners who've maintained residence in Europe or Britain for at least six months. If you're doing a year-long study abroad, you will probably make the cut-off in time for spring break. One benefit of the InterRail pass is that it covers more than both Eurail and Britrail combined. All told, it permits travel in 27 countries, including Britain, Ireland, Morocco and several eastern European countries.

Unlike Eurail and Britrail, InterRail is broken up into 7 zones, each of which contains three or four neighboring countries. Students can buy a ticket covering one, two or three zones, or they can buy a Global Pass, which covers all zones. A one zone ticket for 15 days is £189, a two zone ticket for one month is £224, a 3 zone ticket for one month is £249 and a Global Pass for one month is £279.

Spring Break Stories: Tripped Up!

Two years ago, I attended school for a year in England. For spring break, three friends and I decided to leave the drizzly chill of England and visit Spain's warm southern beaches. We had two weeks of freedom from essays and research papers and wanted to take full advantage of it.

My boyfriend and I bought a used car because we thought it would be cheaper than renting one for two weeks, plus we'd have it for the rest of the year. The four of us packed our stuff and bought travel insurance too, just in case something went wrong.

We set out early for the coast, where would board the ferry to cross the English Channel. We made it only a few miles past London when the car overheated and died. We called the insurance people and after pronouncing it "dead," they gave us a voucher to rent a car for the duration of the trip. The rental car was much nicer than ours and had a stereo, which ours didn't. We transferred all our things to the new car, popped in a remix version of the Pet Shop Boys, and peeled out of the parking lot, trying to make the 9 p.m. ferry.

We arrived in Paris without incident and stopped to see some of the highlights. It was dusk when we stopped at the Eiffel Tower, which was beautiful against the night sky. My boyfriend and I shared a special moment there and I set down my camera to give him my full attention. When I turned back a minute later, it was gone. It had been only a few inches from me!

It takes a long time to drive to Spain. We stayed at funny little hotels and bought cans of ravioli at the grocery store to save money. We also drove on the winding back roads, so we wouldn't be obliged to pay tolls on the main highways. We saw snug French villages and magnificent countryside. We drove though the French Riviera and couldn't afford anything but the view. We got out of the car at a wide place in the road near Cannes and walked a few hundred yards to look at the water. When we returned five minutes later, someone had tried to break in, and the lock on the passenger side of the car was busted. Nothing was taken, however.

We continued on through the French Alps and finally, we arrived in Barcelona, Spain, city of the Olympics, amazing architecture and cultural magnificence. We stayed in a small hostel downtown on a Saturday night. When we woke the next morning, the morning we were to leave and drive farther south, my boyfriend and I wanted to visit a market we had seen and go to services at a lovely old church a few blocks away. Our friends were still tired and wanted to sleep a while longer, so my boyfriend and I put our things in the car, which was parked just down the road beside the church. We noticed that during the night someone else had tried to break in and the driver-side lock was broken. We were disturbed, but were late for the church service.

When we returned to the car two hours later, we found the small side window smashed and our bags gone. The thief, or thieves in all likelihood, didn't get anything of value. Our credit cards and money and passports we kept with us at all times. But still, I sat down on the sidewalk and cried that they had taken my underwear (I had just bought some nice silk underwear), my journal from the trip, my brand-new hiking boots and the *Let's Go Spain* guidebook we had spent most of the previous day looking for!

We stuffed a pillow in the broken window and started back to England. We didn't feel we had any other options. The woman at the car rental agency said she wouldn't trade us cars and cursed at us in Spanish. We knew we would be robbed again if we stayed with that broken window. And we had no clothes, or anything! We boarded the ferry for the return trip and when we got off, my friend realized she didn't have her camera with her. Somehow, it was misplaced on the ferry. So we have no pictures of our ill-fated trip.

We spent the remainder of our spring break in England's beautiful Lake District, where everyone leave things unlocked because there is no fear of robbery.

Alita Byrd
Columbia Union College '97
Takoma Park, Maryland

Relax, Will Ya?

Explore your inner self, awaken your creative spirit, attain a higher consciousness and practice physical, mental and emotional wellness. These lofty goals represent the cornerstones of the annual "Alternative Spring Break" weeks held at the Ananda Kannan Ozark Retreat Center in Willow Springs Missouri. Begun in 1994, these retreats focus on a developing a peaceful, healthy lifestyle through meditation, yoga, sports, vegetarianism and community service. Many participants hail from "Renaissance Universal" clubs, which further the same yogic principles on college campuses. Still, individuals with no Renaissance Universal affiliation are welcome. About 50 students attend the alternative spring break retreat each week it is offered.

The Ananda Kannan Center sponsors two to four consecutive spring break retreats every March. The Ananda Vrati Quest Center in northeastern Pennsylvania and the Ananda Dhiira Center in northern California may also sponsor single retreats. In 1997, the cost of a 5 day, 5 night retreat (transportation not included) was $155. For more information, call 1-800-896-2387.

Freakin' Out at Freaknik

The first Freaknik was a picnic, a simple gathering of about fifty African-American students from a handful of Atlanta-area colleges. That was back in 1982. Today, you won't find picnic blankets or plastic forks at Freaknik. That's because it's grown into the biggest African-American student party around and today takes place as much in the streets and clubs of Atlanta as the green space. In the mid-nineties, sometimes more than 200,000 students would converge for the event, which takes place the third week in April. In the past two years, however the numbers have stayed closer to 100,000.

Happenings & Events

Freaknik, like most spring break events, is largely about scoping out, flirting with and picking up members of the opposite sex; in clubs, at concerts and even in traffic. It's not unusual for Freaknik revelers to abandon their cars to strike a pose or break into dance before a crowd of camera-clicking onlookers. Such practices have given Freaknik a reputation for spunk, spontaneity and gridlock. Not surprisingly, hundreds of traffic tickets are doled out each year.

At Freakniks past, artists such as MC Lyte, 2 Live Crew and 95 South have performed at local arenas. Clubs such as Club E.S.S.O., Patty Hut Café, Club Kaya, 112 and Club Prestige also sponsor live music and special events for Freaknik. The annual step show sponsored by nine fraternities and sororities has also become a favorite among party-goers.

Freaknik.com
http://www.freaknik.com

Want the scoop on Freaknik? This stylish site hands it over on a multi-media platter. There is a five part video interview about Freaknik's history, a photo gallery, an events listing (from Freaknik '97), a public bulletin board and the Freaknik store.

Music Festivals

South by Southwest Music Festival (SXSW)

http://www.sxsw.com/sxsweek.html

Held in Austin, Texas every March, hundreds of unsigned alternative bands perform at local clubs and the Austin Convention Center during this five-day musical extravaganza. In the '97 lineup were such rising stars as The Boo Radleys, Cake, Soul Coughing and Matthew Sweet. Most bands however, are hardly known, coming straight from the garage or the hole-in-the-wall bar. For many of them, SXSW is their big chance to get signed, or at least get noticed; crawling as it is with industry execs, scouts and promoters. For the fans, SXSW is a chance to glimpse alternative music's "next big thing" before it's buffed and polished for the mainstream audience.

While SXSW can be a music-lovers nirvana, tickets are downright hard to come by these days. It's become so popular in recent years that promoters have stopped marketing it nationally. Now, the only way to get tickets without registering for the accompanying multimedia conference and independent film festival, too (at a cost of over $300), is to buy them in Austin about a week before the event. At SXSW '97, wrist-bands, good for entry into most shows, cost $60. SXSW '98 is set for March 13-22.

Canadian Music Week (CMW)

http://www.nor.com/music.cmw/cmw.htm
This week-long Toronto music festival features over four hundred up-and-coming Canadian artists in every genre from rock and hip hop to jazz and bluegrass. Like SXSW, it is a major showcase for hot young bands and a premiere scout-fest for record industry honchos. Past CMWs, have launched such bands as The Tragically Hip and The Monoxides, bringing them into the national (Canadian) spotlight.

Canadian Music Week takes place every March and runs concurrently with the Canadian Music Conference and the Music and Multimedia Show. At CMW '97, wristbands allowing admission into all concert venues cost $30. For tickets, call 416-695-9236.

The Road Trip

Ahhhh Fandango! Nothing sums up the college road like this 1985 movie starring Kevin Costner and Judd Nelson. With a few friends, they set off down the highway for one last rollicking good time before their college days end and responsibility sets in. Eventually, they get just what they're after, breakdowns and bickering notwithstanding. It's not a hard act to follow, just takes a penchant for adventure and a love of the road. Try it, you'll see.

Below are just a few cities that might make interesting stops this spring break. Some are good for a week's stay, others for a day's. Several are in the winter coat zone, but a few will meet the snowbird's standards, too. The list is by no means complete, and it's not meant to be. Rather, it's meant to whet your palate, pique your curiosity and get you in the road rambling mood.

Las Vegas, Nevada

There's no doubt that Las Vegas is the queen of all money-inhaling cities. Its massive neon lights and super-glam casinos are simply reprocessed tourist dollars, after all. Still, it's a perennial favorite with spring breakers. An oxymoron? Not necessarily, as Las Vegas vacations are amazingly inexpensive when gambling instincts are kept in check. That's because casinos subsidize food and lodging costs to attract the high-rolling masses. Hotel rooms are dirt cheap if you go the four-to-a-room route, while filling buffet meals can go for as little as $3 for breakfast and $6 for dinner. Plus, as long as you're putting money in the slots or playing the tables, drinks (alkie and non) are free. In short, Las Vegas is a low-budget blast if you can keep a handle on your cash card. Besides, where else can you travel to Camelot, Oz, Ancient Rome, Egypt and New York City all in one day?

New Orleans, Louisiana

Another favorite spring break destination, New Orleans is most often associated with Mardi Gras, jazz and jambalaya. All three are good reasons to visit. If you have an early spring break, hit town for Mardi Gras, the largest bead-throwing, mask-wearing, parade-watching fête around. (In 1998, Mardi Gras is February 24, though the partying starts about 2 weeks earlier.) If your spring break is later, you might be lucky enough to catch Super Sunday, which usually falls on the Sunday closest to March 19 (St. Joseph's Day). On this day, elaborately costumed "gangs" with names like Wild Magnolias and Golden Star Hunters parade through Crescent City neighborhoods singing to the boisterous rhythms of drums and tambourines. The event is considered to be the back-street answer to Mardi Gras.

Memphis, Tennessee

This is one of the few places you'll find peanut butter and banana sandwiches featured on a restaurant menu. The reason for this anomaly? Easy, the city's most celebrated native son liked 'em. You know, that Presley guy. Naturally, Memphis has capitalized on its Elvis renown, building Graceland into a monster tourist attraction. If you can stomach a little commercialism, you'll appreciate this monument to the original hip-swiveling dervish. If nothing else, go to satisfy your curiosity. Before you bust town, stop at Sun Studio, where such musical greats as Roy Orbison, B.B. King and Hank Williams got started.

Atlanta, Georgia

It's an emerging metropolis, home to a number of major corporations and all of their marketing machinery. To see an impressive display of corporate advertising, check out the vast World of Coca Cola. There, you'll follow the progress of our favorite over-hyped soft drink, from its humble beginnings in 1886 to its current status as cola king. Not only will you get to drink your fill of Coke, you'll get to sample Coca Cola Corp. drinks from all over the world. Next, consider a trip to CNN's headquarters. "All news, all the time" is more interesting than it sounds. Take the forty-minute walking tour and you'll get a behind-the-scenes look at Headline News, CNN International and CNN Interactive (web-based news.) If you're lucky, you'll catch a glimpse of network talking heads in action. (Call 404-827-2300 for tour reservations.)

Cleveland, Ohio

Granted, Cleveland can still give you a mean case of the wintertime blues in March. But there are rewards for those willing to put on their mittens and stick it out. First among these is the Rock and Roll Hall of Fame, a dazzling high-tech shrine to this unique musical medium and all its faithful practitioners. You'll see such predictable rock-star paraphernalia as Michael Jackson's glove and John Lennon's Sergeant Pepper jacket, but better are the bigger exhibits showcasing bands and chronicling seminal rock events. Running through spring '98 is the Hall of Fame's first temporary exhibit, "I Want to Take You Higher," a look at rock and social culture in the age of psychedelics.

Seattle, Washington

As the capital of coffee and the mecca of microbrew, Seattle knows well how to wake up, wind down and just generally hang out. Thus, it's a natural choice for the footloose fun-hunter looking for a funky place to spend a few days. If you need to indulge your tourist instincts, go ahead and climb the Space Needle. The view from 518 feet is indeed impressive. Next, ramble around quirky Fremont, an area known for retro clothing and vintage furniture stores, art galleries and Seattle's favorite public artwork, *Waiting for the Interurban*. Finally, don't leave Seattle, land of Nirvana, Pearl Jam and Alice in Chains, without exploring its thriving musical scene. The city's clubs hop with live acts every night. Try the Crocodile Cafe, Backstage, OK Cafe, Doc Maynard's, Showbox Lounge, Fenix/Fenix Underground, or Sit and Spin. Also, don't forget to pay your respects to Jimi Hendrix at his grave site outside of town.

Vancouver, British Columbia

Located 140 miles north of Seattle, Vancouver is a lively and eclectic city, appropriately nicknamed Hollywood North because so many movies and television shows are filmed there. Calling all X-Files fans! Take a tour of the city and you can relive hundreds of Scully and Mulder moments: at the dry docks near Lonsdale Quay, the rail yards at the edge of Gastown, the cruise ship terminal at Canada Place, the University of British Columbia campus, the Plaza of the Nations and the art-deco Marine Building, to name a few. If you're lucky, maybe you'll happen on a live shoot. If you're not, head to Vancouver's bustling Chinatown for a heap of consoling egg rolls. Continue the fit of self-indulgence on the chic Robson Street shopping strip, or escape from it all in the 5-story IMAX movie theater at Canada Place.

Spring Break Stories: Canada is an Exotic, Foreign Land

In the *USA Today* weather map of life, most people choose to spend their spring breaks somewhere orange, or at least yellow. Not me. I didn't even hang around somewhere blue. I went all the way to the white zone. I went to Canada.

Why Canada? My friends and I evaluated all of the places we could go for spring break. We weighed the pros and cons of each carefully, eliminating anywhere that advertised with photos of women skiing in bikinis and decided to go to Canada for many important reasons:

1. It is a foreign land.
2. It is easy to find.

To get to Canada from the University of South Dakota, we drove north through South Dakota (state motto: "There's a reason you've never been this far north before."), continued through North Dakota (state motto: "There is nothing to see for miles, perhaps because of the three-inch layer of frost on the car window") and passed through Canadian customs (Customs motto: "We hate you.")

The customs people tried to act scary and asked a bunch of questions, but they had no way of knowing if we were lying. They probably don't care, because if they caught someone doing something illegal, they'd have to walk out of their heated booths and risk loosing limbs in the Canadian cold.

Once we were in the country, we decided Canada has several exotic characteristics. One native told us Canada has two seasons. There's "so-cold-the-even-polar-bears-don't want-to-go-outside," and then there's "mosquitos-the-size-of-Buicks-will-suck-you-dry" season.

So Canada can be a frightening foreign land if you spend any time outside of a climate-controlled, mosquito-free environment like The Gap. Canadians have thought up several ways to amuse themselves while they are trapped indoors all year long, such as rewriting all of their signs in French and using silly words like "odour" and "centre."

We stayed in Winnipeg, which boasts numerous cultural attractions, such as the Royal Winnipeg Ballet, the Winnipeg Art Gallery and the Manatoba Theater Center. Of course, we skipped all of these for two important reasons:

1. The drinking age in Canada is 18.
2. We were 19.

I highly recommend Canada to the spring break traveler. If you can avoid being frozen or sucked dry, you will have a very good time. Just try to keep your sense of humour.

Karen Barker
University of South Dakota '97
Vermillion, SD

Web Site Index

Part I – Beach Breaks

MTV .... http://www.mtv.com
Sun Shine Magazine .... http://interoz.com/springbreak/
SpringBreak.com .... http://www.springbreak.com
R&J's Spring Break Resource Page .... http://ccwf.cc.utexas.edu/~guard/
springbreak.htm
MapQuest .... http://www.mapquest.com/

Greyhound Bus Lines .... http://www.greyhound.com/
Amtrak Railway .... http://www.amtrak.com/
Breakaway Tours .... http://www.breakawaytours.com
Inter-Campus Programs .... http://www.icpt.com
Student Travel Services .... http://www.ststravel.com

Take A Break Student Travel .... http://www.takeabreak.com/
Sun Splash Tours .... http://www.sunsplashtours.com
Sunchase Tours .... http://www.sunchase.com
Vagabond Tours .... http://vagabondtours.com
Bacchus and Gamma .... http://bacchusgamma.org

Panama City Beach .... http://interoz.com/pcb
Welcome to Panama City Beach .... http://www.travelfile.com/get?pcbeach
Daytona Beach Spring Break http://www.1idea.com/daytonabreak/
Spring Break Photo Essay .... http://www.journale.com/SPRBREAK/
springbreakintro.html
The Elbo Cam .... http://www.justsurfit.com/elboroom
/cam1.shtml

The City of Fort Lauderdale Online .... http://info.ci.ftlaud.fl.us/
Greater Fort Lauderdale Convention
and Visitors Bureau .... http://www.co.broward.fl.us/sunny.htm
Key West Online http://www.vacation3.com/
Key West Paradise .... http://www.keywestparadise.com/
Key West FAQ .... http://members.aol.com/KeyWestFAQ/
index.html

Gay Key West .... http://www.gaykeywestfl.com/
South Padre Island Convention
and Visitors Bureau .... http://www.sopadre.com

The Alternative South Padre Island Page .... http://www.south-padre-island.com
Sons of the Beach .... http://www.unlitter.com
Lake Havasu Virtual Community .... http://www.lakehavasucity.com
Lake Havasu City Community Pages .... http://www.havasu.com/
Lake Havasu City Convention & Visitors
   Bureau .... http://www.amdest.com/az/LHC/
                                    LHCCVB/vacation.html

Kennedy Space Center Office of Public
   Affairs .... http://www-pao.ksc.nasa.gov/kscpao/
                                    kscpao.htm
Major League Baseball .... http://www.majorleaguebaseball.com/
                                    springtraining/
Cancún .... http://www.yucatanweb.com/
Cancún: The User's Guide .... http://www.caribe.net.mx/siegel/
                                    nofrdir.htm
Jamaican Tourist Board .... http://www.jamaicatravel.com

De Site on Jamaica .... http://www.jamaicans.com/jam.htm
The Bahamas Official Travel Guide .... http://www.interknowledge.com/
                                    bahamas/bshome01.htm
The Bahamas .... http://thebahamas.com/

Part II – Slopeside Breaks

Moguls Ski and Snowboard Tours .... http://www.skimoguls.com/
Sports America Tours .... http://sportsamerica.com
Sunchase Tours .... http://www.sunchase.com
Breakaway Tours .... http://www.breakawaytours.com
Student Adventure Travel .... http://www.studentadvtrav.com

SkiNet .... http://www.skinet.com/
Ski Central .... http://skicentral.com
GoSki .... http://www.goski.com
Snowboardz.com .... http://www.snowboardz.com/
Frost .... http://www.charged.com/frost

Beauty .... http://www.beauty.se/
Killington .... http://www.killington.com
Stowe .... http://www.stowe.com
Tremblant .... http://www.goski.com/rcan/trembla.htm
Mont-Sainte-Anne .... http://www.goski.com/rcan/mtsa.htm

Steamboat .... http://www.steamboat-ski.com
Crested Butte .... http://www.toski.com/crested/
Breckenridge .... http://www.ski-breckenridge.com/
                                    breck.html

Part III – Trail Breaks

Part IV – Spring Break Alternatives

Habitat For Humanity .... http://www.habitat.org
Vanderbilt University ASB .... http://osiris.vuse.vanderbilt.edu/asb/
asb.htm
Stanford University .... http://www.stanford.edu
University of Michigan .... http://www.umich.edu/~ocsl/asb/
index.html
Oxfam America .... http://www.charity.org/oxfam.html

Christmas in April .... http://www.pdi.com/cina-usa/index.html
Break Away: The Alternative Break
Connection .... http://www.vanderbilt.edu/breakaway
Who Cares? A Journal of Service
and Action .... http://www.whocares.org
COOL (Campus Outreach Opportunity
League) http://www.cool2serve.org
SERVEnet .... http://www.servenet.org/

Let's Go Guides .... http://hsa.net/travel
Berkeley Guides .... http://www.fodors.com
Lonely Planet Guides .... http://www.lonelyplanet.com
Eurail .... http://www.eurail.com/
BritRail .... http://www.eurail.com/britrail/

Freaknik.com .... http://www.freaknik.com
South by Southwest Music Festival .... http://www.sxsw.com/sxsweek.html
Canadian Music Week.................................... http://www.vaxxine.com/cmw